TEN MEDITATIONS FOR CATCHING AND LOSING ONE'S BREATH

I0197838

KALOS

The word *kalos* (καλός) means beautiful. It is the call of the good; that which arouses interest, desire: "I am here." Beauty brings the appetite to rest at the same time as it wakens the mind from its daily slumber, calling us to look afresh at that which is before our very eyes. It makes virgins of us all, and of everything—there, before us, lies something that we never noticed before. Beauty consists in *integritas sive perfectio* (integrity and perfection) and *claritas* (brightness/clarity). It is the reason why we rise and why we sleep—that great night of dependence, one that reveals the borrowed existence of all things, if, that is, there is to be a thing at all, or if there is to be a person at all. Here lies the ground of all science, of philosophy, and of all theology, indeed of our each and every day.

This series will seek to provide intelligent-yet-accessible volumes that have the innocence of beauty and of true adventure, and in so doing remind us all again of that which we took for granted, most of all thought itself.

SERIES EDITORS:
Conor Cunningham, Eric Austin Lee, and Christopher Ben Simpson

Ten Meditations for Catching and Losing One's Breath

. . .

BY Jean-Louis Chrétien

TRANSLATED BY
Steven DeLay

WITH A FOREWORD BY
Emmanuel Housset

CASCADE *Books* · Eugene, Oregon

TEN MEDITATIONS FOR CATCHING AND LOSING ONE'S BREATH

Kalos series

Copyright © 2024 Steven DeLay. All rights reserved. Except for brief quotations in critical publications or reviews, no part of this book may be reproduced in any manner without prior written permission from the publisher. Write: Permissions, Wipf and Stock Publishers, 199 W. 8th Ave., Suite 3, Eugene, OR 97401.

Cascade Books
An Imprint of Wipf and Stock Publishers
199 W. 8th Ave., Suite 3
Eugene, OR 97401

www.wipfandstock.com

PAPERBACK ISBN: 978-1-6667-6611-0
HARDCOVER ISBN: 978-1-6667-6612-7
EBOOK ISBN: 978-1-6667-6613-4

Cataloguing-in-Publication data:

Names: Chrétien, Jean-Louis [author]. | DeLay, Steven [translator]. | Housset, Emmanuel, [foreword writer].

Title: Ten Meditations for catching and losing one's breath / by Jean-Louis Chrétien ; translated by Steven DeLay ; foreword by Emmanuel Housset.

Description: Eugene, OR: Cascade Books, 2024 | Series: Kalos | Includes bibliographical references.

Identifiers: ISBN 978-1-6667-6611-0 (paperback) | ISBN 978-1-6667-6612-7 (hardcover) | ISBN 978-1-6667-6613-4 (ebook)

Subjects: LCSH: Meditation. | Bible—Reading. | Spiritual life—Christianity.| Bible—Devotional use. | Phenomenology. | Language and languages—Philosophy.

Classification: BS617 C474 2024 (paperback) | BS617 (ebook)

VERSION NUMBER 08/14/24

Contents

Foreword | vii

About the Author and Translator | xii

Translator's Introduction | xiii

Preface | xix

Meditation 1: Breath | 1

Meditation 2: Way | 11

Meditation 3: Temptation | 22

Meditation 4: Attention | 33

Meditation 5: Recollection | 44

Meditation 6: Blessing | 54

Meditation 7: Peace | 63

Meditation 8: Gentleness | 73

Meditation 9: Abandonment | 83

Meditation 10: Wound | 94

Foreword

WOUNDED EXISTENCE

JEAN-LOUIS CHRÉTIEN IS UNDOUBTEDLY one of the great philosophers of our time, and his breathless and restless speech has itself trained a number of important researchers, and transformed many lives by opening a pathway to the wound of being. Even if he cultivated discretion and did not seek honors, even if his thought did not live amid the spirit of the times and knew how to remain philosophical, which is to say untimely (which does not mean irrelevant), his own journey unfurls in more than thirty works from *Lueur du secret* (1985), to *Fragilité* (2017), without forgetting the posthumous work *Parole et poésie* (2023). A group of his closest friends, notably Pierre Carrique, Jérôme Laurent, and Camille Riquier, are responsible for making certain of his articles available again and for making accessible his archives, which are deposited at the Institut Mémoires de l'Edition Contemporaine (IMEC) at the Ardenne Abbey near the town of Caen, which is a privileged place of work for young researchers. Thus, a few years after his death, Chrétien has already become a "classic" figure.

Of course, an author's biography says nothing about his philosophy, and even risks missing his most incisive theses. Chrétien abhorred the very project of "contextualizing" a thought, which in turn no longer is described as thinking and becomes a mere encyclopedia entry. That said, it is important to note that he had a career of excellence, first at the Ecole Normale Supérieure in Paris beginning with the philosophy aggregation. After a few years of teaching secondary school and having defended his thesis, *L'herméneutique de l'obliquité dans le néoplatonisme et le christianisme antiques*, he became a young lecturer at the University of Créteil, near Paris, where I had the privilege of having him supervise my master's thesis and prepare me for the philosophy aggregation the following year. In 1988, he took a position at the Sorbonne University (Paris IV) teaching ancient philosophy, and after obtaining his Habilitation to direct research, he became a professor there, holding the chair of "Antiquité tardive et philosophie médiévale." At the Sorbonne, he was able to work with the best in each field of philosophy in France, as he liked to say, and to train several generations of students in the rigorous reading of texts and in listening to the truth. One can tell a tree by its fruit, and in many of today's philosophers we can detect the hallmark of his exacting standards, conscientiousness, and his thinking about the elusiveness of manifestation. His learnedness was immense, and he knew how to integrate Greek philosophy, medieval philosophy, biblical hermeneutics, systematic theology, phenomenology, the philosophy of art, literature, and poetry.

Marked deeply by the work of Heidegger, but also by Henri Maldiney, whom he knew personally, he always sought erudition in the history of philosophy, while knowing not to allow himself to be enslaved by it, so that he might develop his own investigation of the ordeal of beauty, night, fatigue, love, and call and fragility, all with an eye to describing an ipseity that always transcends itself, and that receives itself from what gives itself to it. In this reflection on all of the phenomenon's dimensions and gradations, he always saw himself as very near to Jean-Luc Marion's philosophy, developing a philosophical vocabulary that beats in virtue of its being animated by the elsewhere. In light of these two considerations, the essence of life is not something that seeks to preserve itself, or that experiences and desires only itself, but gives itself by responding to a situation's call.

Classifying his work as "Christian philosophy" is beside the point, and he never called himself a Christian philosopher, thus avoiding all the old controversies associated with the term. Chrétien's project is not to justify Christianity philosophically, which does not need it, and he has always strictly distinguished the lights of reason and of faith. Nonetheless, all his work seeks to show that there indeed is a philosophy in Christianity whose listening makes possible one of the most radical challenges to the metaphysics of subjectivity as a closed, self-grounding, autotelic subjectivity; even more radical than Nietzsche's. If there is such a thing as training in Christianity, to borrow a Kierkegaardian expression Chrétien has commented on extensively, it is because it gives thought to an ipseity wounded by the ordeal of that which exceeds it, of that which uncovers without uncovering itself. The naked soul, according to Chrétien, is one that lives from elsewhere, from the proximity of the distant, and for which the unhoped-for can be its horizon of presence. Chrétien's work as a whole seeks to elucidate this figure of selfhood other than the one arising from the a priori capacity for reflection alone: it is there where I forget myself, and do not seek to safeguard what is mine, that I can become myself. The naked voice is one wounded by an elsewhere, a trembling voice that still yet strives to respond. Our true humanity resides in this voice, which this book, *Ten Meditations for Catching and Losing One's Breath*, invites us to bear without fear of flagging, for it is the call of being that keeps us moving. Chrétien in this book develops a hermeneutic of finitude that underscores the agonic dimension of wholly exposed, naked existence. Our fragile, fleeting existence can be offered up, and it is in this gift that a dimension of eternity lies. The most fragile receives the most solid, the most temporal the most eternal.

Ten Meditations for Catching and Losing One's Breath is intended, then, as a reminder of philosophy's indebtedness to words. For if it is in words that we think, it is also words that make us think, that open our eyes to being, rather than being a mere garment thrown over it. In the very depths of its sedimented layers, speech gives meaning its linguistic flesh, as Husserl said, and this linguistic flesh is what we must learn to respect so as never to distort phenomena. Word by word, these *ten brief meditations* ([*dix brèves méditations*] as the book is subtitled in French) enable us to learn to pay attention to words, giving us the "flexibility" to adjust to the phenomenon, rather than trying to adjust it to us or to an extrinsic measure. By showing us how to enroll ourselves in the school of words, which are the principles of their own apprehension, this phenomenology makes suppleness the very condition of respect for the phenomenon. More still, listening to this linguistic flesh is what gives us our own flesh, one that is not primarily a matter of reflexivity, but of exposure to the world, as it is through this that we can exist by suffering for the truth. It is no coincidence that the last word of these meditations meant to set us on our way is "wound."

Nothing is more foreign to Chrétien than the notion of a linguistic turn in philosophy, as this would paradoxically be the apogee of the severing of word and thing, and for him, these ten brief meditations on speech consist in taking up a constitutive theme of philosophy ever since its Platonic birth: listening to words is the birth of philosophy, because it is the very opening to the world. Thus, the ten words chosen by Chrétien are precisely not words to speak merely to oneself, but are living words of interpersonal commonality, and this is why they help to elucidate that figure of selfhood so ancient and so new: it is where I give myself, where I abandon myself in trust, that I truly become myself. These ten words accordingly describe ten acts, not of the self, but of being oneself in the nudity of existence, in being exposed to the elsewhere. Each word is a way, says Chrétien in his preface, a path that leads from the world to the other, to others who pave our future. By overcoming the forgetting of words, which is a forgetting of things also, we overcome the forgetting of others as well, and ultimately the forgetting of ourselves. Indeed, these words are not categories of understanding, nor do they belong to a conceptual language, which loses all the richness of being in an obsession with external univocity, and misses the fabric of words and things. They are, therefore, inherited words whose reactivation provides the lifeblood of our thinking. The philosopher's task, then, is to make these words audible again, so that we do not remain mute in the face of the world, whether in its violence or its beauty. Consequently, to elucidate the word is not to make it transparent, but to reveal what is irreducible in it, to restore to it the power to transform and to metamorphize our existence. Philosophical thought does not aim to neutralize the alterity of words, but to enable us to think by way of them, in order to rediscover the otherness of the world and ourselves. There is an acquiescence to words that makes possible the concept, and it is this "lesson in words"[1] that Chrétien gives us to think. He teaches us, thus, to think by weighing our words carefully, so that they lead us to our natural place, the phenomena.

All ten of these words, and above all the word *breath*, teach us that our life is not sufficient to itself, but is a continual exchange of interiority and of exteriority through which we are also born according to the spirit. To be oneself is to be able to receive the gentle breeze of the spirit's breath and to transmit it through our fragility, thus making it ripen and bear fruit. Hence, the *way* is a journey, a style all our own, but it is not charted in advance, and it is the one who receives himself from elsewhere who can go further rather than trampling about and dallying. That said, every *way* is steep and is tested by *temptation*, which is a situation, an encounter, putting us a question. By deciding on the meaning of what happens to us, we discover ourselves in the ordeal and in the patience of hope. It is through temptations that one becomes a person and develops *attention*, which is a work of the mind and spirit respecting the time of phenomena. This attention is freedom's fulfillment, because it sets and leaves us free, in the twofold sense of open-mindedness and devotion. This leads to *recollection*, which

1. Here I quote Jérôme de Gramont in his review of Chrétien's book, *Nunc* 20, February 2010.

is not a state, but an act of freeing oneself from the preoccupation with self-mastery. Recollection comes from the encounters themselves and is at once the presence to itself and the affected being of the naked soul. In turn, gestures of *blessing* are those that say "yes," and the desire for a benediction is already itself a blessing, because it delivers us from self-imprisonment. Consequently, making *peace* is an endless task, and it is every day that we make progress on the path to it. It is the fruit of charity, the work of love. It implies accepting doing violence to oneself in order to let increase within oneself a pacifying force that is not our own. The whole book converges on the analysis of *gentleness*, which is the "how" of personal existence. Speech's gentleness presupposes the patience of listening, and in this respect, it is a receptivity to the fragility of things and people. Blessed are the meek, for they do not brutalize phenomena, words, or people, and it is this slow, penetrating gentleness that makes possible inhabiting the earth. In this phenomenology of selfhood describing its constitutive flexibility, *abandonment* is always entwined with trust, and involves abandoning everything of the world and oneself so as to surrender oneself to others and to God. To be oneself, to become a person, means learning little by little to be free of oneself, to be free for something other than oneself, to be available to the call of every situation. And so, a *wound* is the penetration of us by something higher than ourselves. The wound of love is what saves us; it is what renders us supple and generous. It is our future.

These ten brief meditations show that Chrétien's philosophy is itself always in transit, and does not allow itself to be hemmed into a single doctrine. By letting us hear how the words of ordinary language can be enflamed by an otherworldliness irreducible to our a priori capacities, and carry a future of significance that has a force of destiny, Chrétien gives us a task of patience and hope, of listening and speaking. Providing us a grasp of the unheard content of these ten words, he returns us to ourselves, to our common task of responding with our whole lives, right up to our last breath. The true philosopher is not a smooth talker who seduces credulous minds, but one who teaches us to read, listen, and speak, and so sets us free for truth itself.

Emmanuel Housset

About the Author and Translator

Jean-Louis Chrétien was a French poet and philosopher. The author of thirty books, his philosophical work in 2012 was the recipient of the inaugural Prix du Cardinal Lustiger from the Académie Française. He was emeritus professor of philosophy at Sorbonne University at the time of his death in 2019.

Steven DeLay is an Old Member of Christ Church, University of Oxford. He is the author of philosophical works and works of fiction, including *Elijah Newman Died Today* (2022) and *Faint Not* (2022).

Translator's Introduction

BEHIND ANY GREAT PHILOSOPHICAL or spiritual work there lies an origin. No single account that anyone might attempt to offer could hope to convey the story of that genesis completely, yet despite the partiality and incompleteness that is inevitably sure to beset an account of the work's birth, a word on the matter can be illuminating nonetheless. This is true not only with respect to the story of the work's first appearing in its original form, but also of the subsequent rebirth it undergoes through its appearance in translations. The appearance of Jean-Louis Chrétien's *Pour reprendre et perdre haleine: Dix brèves méditations* in English, entitled here as *Ten Meditations for Catching and Losing One's Breath*, is no exception.

Originally published in French in 2009 with Bayard, it is the labor of an author whose thinking was by then as well-regarded as it was well-established for its unique voice and unrivaled erudition. Among Anglophone readers, Chrétien's name had come to become closely associated with the philosophical movement of phenomenology, owing to the fact that his work had been designated, in the early nineties, by Dominique Janicaud under the umbrella of the "theological turn" in French phenomenology. Along with a number of other French philosophers such as Emmanuel Levinas, Paul Ricœur, Michel Henry, and Jean-Luc Marion (and later Jean-Yves Lacoste and Emmanuel Falque), Chrétien was responsible for revitalizing and reimagining the legacy of Husserl and Heidegger. In works of his that have been available in English for a while now, including *The Unforgettable and the Unhoped For* (2002), *Hand to Hand* (2003), *The Ark of Speech* (2004), and *The Call and the Response* (2004), his philosophical writings contributed significantly to a thoroughgoing refiguration of the phenomenological tradition, challenging and reworking the movement's self-conception by simultaneously testing its limits and expanding its horizons.

Consequently, one might conclude that Chrétien's work is a continuation of the twentieth-century Parisian phenomenologists before him, most notably Sartre and Merleau-Ponty. However, as his taken surname suggests (*Chrétien* is French for "Christian"), it would be impossible to reduce Chrétien's vision to the secular phenomenological milieu preceding it. To begin with, his authorship draws on the history of letters expansively, not from phenomenology only, or even from the history of philosophy as a whole, but also from poetry, literature, and theology, especially the patristics and the mystics, and above all his beloved Augustine. Furthermore, and even more fundamentally, Chrétien's is a profoundly spiritual vision. In reading him, one cannot help but be struck immediately by the penetrating, and highly sensitive, nature of his attunement to all that which makes life human, these many small, but important, things that lesser authors do not notice at all, much less explore so illuminatingly. For all its immense erudition and rigor, then, Chrétien's work is most distinctive for its refreshing simplicity and purity, an unaffected sincerity whose style no doubt is the consequence of its author's deep faith, and a form of spiritual commitment that made that authorship a reflection and continuation of that very faith itself. For this reason, even his strictly philosophical or scholarly works are always edifying.

But in the work presented here, Chrétien reduces the matters before him even more radically than he does elsewhere, producing a text meant to embark its reader along a meditative path that attunes us to the subtle riches of the human experience before God. While it is probably best to straightforwardly render the French subtitle's *brève* as "brief," one might justifiably also describe the work's meditations as "succinct," for although they are short, they are fecund, their minimalistic economy of expression plumbing the depths of which they speak.

Although the other works mentioned above have been available to an English audience for some time, that body of translations is only a small portion of the late author's colossal productivity. Over a span of thirty years, beginning with the publication of *Lueur du secret* (1985) and concluding with *Fragilité* (2017), Chrétien authored thirty books, averaging approximately a book a year. Most recently, his literary executors edited and published a volume of collected articles, *Parole et poésie* (2023), that were written over the years. At the time of his death in 2019, he had been working on a new book exploring the phenomenon of absence. That work may eventually be published posthumously also, even though the manuscript was left off unfinished.

Some readers therefore may wonder. Of all of his many works that still remain to be translated into English, why select this one? The answer is that the choice was in a way Chrétien's own. In 2017, while working on my manuscript of *Phenomenology in France* (2019), a text that includes a chapter exploring Chrétien's work, we began a letter correspondence. I had obtained his Paris address from one of the other authors whom that work discusses. Without expecting to receive a response from the man who was so famously private and elusive, I sent Chrétien a draft of the chapter on his work. To my surprise, that August I received a letter from him in reply. The following spring, we met in Paris at the Place de Vosges, where we walked to a café at the Place de Bastille. When we took a seat at the café, he pulled out a copy of *Pour reprendre et perdre haleine* from his backpack, and gave it to me.

As anyone who has read Chrétien knows, his works are remarkable for the immense breadth of texts from which he drew. The sheer number of quotations sometimes on even a single page—and from such a diverse range of sources—is staggering. And yet, Chrétien does not quote haphazardly. He gathered many voices, bringing them together in a way that said something that had not yet been said, and would not otherwise have been said. Hoping to hear directly from him the secret to his method, I asked him how he went about choosing whom to cite, and how he went about arranging the passages from which he quoted. He chuckled, turned to me, and looked up to the sky: "I stare up at the ceiling, and it comes to me." What he was saying, I take it, is that he could not offer a satisfactory explanation of how he was able to write the works he did, other than to say that they were the result of inspiration, which for him meant listening to the Holy Spirit.

Only a few months later, I received what would be my last communication from him. Dated January 4, 2019, he opens the letter by apologizing for a "long silence." He had been busy finalizing a chapter for a book on which he was working (the one on absence). More pressingly, he had been dealing with a mysterious health ailment. He relates having undergone recent periods of intense facial paralysis—"I could no longer speak intelligibly, nor eat anything other than by liquid, and my face became a frozen, expressionless mask." He says that in recent weeks the symptoms had improved, and that he is optimistic the disconcerting episode was only a fleeting issue. However, it proved to be a cancer from which he died just six months later in June.

Since then, when revisiting the pages of *Pour reprendre et perdre haleine*, I have wondered why, of all his many works, this was the one that he chose to give me. Was it a personal favorite of his? Having begun to get to know me through our correspondence, was it a text from which he thought I might personally benefit? Or, was there perhaps nothing particularly conscientious about the choice of gift? After all, his decision to give me a book—much less this specific one—simply may have been a spur-of-the-moment decision on his part, something he did on a whim while literally heading out the door to meet me. I have no way of knowing what particular personal significance, if any, there was to the gesture.

In another of his earlier letters, Chrétien expressed great joy at the anticipation of the forthcoming publication of *Fragilité* with Minuit, as well as *Spacious Joy* (2019) in English. Despite his prolificity, he remained truly grateful, enthusiastic, and appreciative to see a work of his appear in translation, so that new readers might enjoy it. When a great philosopher dies, understandably his body of life's work becomes something that scholars feast upon—the corpus becomes a topic of debate and interpretation. Even this sort of reception pays a kind of homage to the author's work, since the fact it receives the attention that it does implies readers find it worthy of scrutiny and thought. Like his *Under the Gaze of the Bible* (2015), *Ten Meditations for Catching and Losing One's Breath* is a work worthy of attention, it seems to me, because it is Chrétien at his very best, for it unapologetically calls us to grow in the grace of Christ, by encouraging us to grasp the love of the Savior, who, in his love for us, redeemed us by willingly having gone to the cross, where he drew a last breath that, as the author of Hebrews says (2:14), defeated the power of death.

I should like to conclude this brief introduction by thanking Matthew Wimer, Robin Parry, and Zechariah Mickel at Wipf and Stock for the great hospitality they have shown this work, and to Jérôme Laurent and to Camille Ricquier for allowing me to undertake it. I should also like to thank Scott Davidson, John Dunaway, and Stephen E. Lewis for their helpful advice regarding certain matters of translation that protected me from going astray. In keeping with the decision in general to render the French literally, I have preserved the traditional male pronouns of the original French.

My hope is that this work will go some way to delivering Chrétien's voice from what might otherwise be the "long silence" of death, by letting him speak to English readers who have not yet read its words. It must be said that my French is far from perfect. I thus ask the reader to pardon whatever infelicities and blunders the text contains. Nevertheless, I believe it expresses the heart of what Chrétien has said, and even retains something of his voice. Were he here to receive it, I like to believe its appearance in English would have been welcomed in that spirit of joyfulness which was characteristically his, and for which he is fondly remembered.

Steven DeLay

Preface

LADEN WITH HISTORY AND thought, resounding with thousands of voices through which what was most proper to them has been discovered, words, those at least that last and endure, have a weight. This weight of light and of sense ballasts our speech, renders it deep and serious, and this ballast, like that of ships, makes speech capable of unprecedented crossings. The following pages meditate on, and question, ten words that belong to the most ordinary language, and were simultaneously decisive in the spiritual tradition. It is a matter of listening to them, of letting their bulk descend within us, in order to place ourselves on the paths of existence of which they form the promise and sending. How would it be possible to do it alone, deafening oneself to those who measured themselves against and by them? Poets and mystics, philosophers too, knowing what speech seeks to say, which is to say, never ceasing to learn from it, are here the masters of attention. This attention is always focused on what these words can make of us, and for us, on what they open to our existence, and without which we could not have found the way, or at least not before many obscure trials and errors. Each of these words is a path.

To say this is to state what this book is not and does not intend to be. It is neither a lexicon or a dictionary, nor is it an academic and historical study of the destiny of these words. No specialized knowledge is presupposed here, and the meditations aim to introduce that about which they speak. References have been provided in the simplest way in the body of the text parenthetically, permitting anyone who wishes to refer to their source to do so, without overwhelming the reader with a whole apparatus of notes.[1]

---

1. Chrétien himself does not append any notes in the original, and thus all those to follow are the translator's own. They have been kept to a minimum, either to clarify a matter of translation, to cite other works of Chrétien relevant to the matter at hand, to provide brief yet essential context, or else simply to introduce and clarify Chrétien's interlocutor who, sufficiently obscure, warrants explication. Trans.

The progression is from the most general to the specific, yet the chapters each form a vessel of autonomous meaning, and so can be read in isolation. I am responsible for translations when no name is mentioned, with the exception of biblical quotations, which usually follow the translation of the most recent edition of the so-called Jerusalem Bible, without any particular indication (even if it is I who sometimes translate verses from the New Testament). Some linguistic traces bear the mark of the finitude of my competences, but this book aims to be European.

The meditations often evoke the unexpected, and I owe it to the reader to say that I had not planned the work. It was fortuitous, something unforeseen by even me. Its initiative derives from the friendly request of Mrs. Claude Plettner and Mr. Frédéric Boyer, who, having convinced me to write "Breath" (*Souffle*) and "Recollection" (*Recueillement*), did not stop there. May they be thanked! They are the ones who set reasonable parameters for the chapter lengths, but it goes without saying that complete freedom over the choice of the other words was left to me. As it was not a question of repeating analyses that I could undertake in other books, this freedom was guided by a concern to approach new themes. One therefore should not be surprised by the omission of words that are dear to me, such as "word" and "speech" (*parole*), "silence," or "joy." The tone of this book is less equanimous than its table of contents may suggest, for to talk of peace is also to speak of war, and to talk of meekness is also to speak of what conquers. In some cases, a very precise angle of approach has been adopted, which is why, for example, the chapter on "blessing" is devoted to that which is torn out by the force of insistence and importunity.

The title clearly indicates this book's intent. Words want our voice and, above all, our breath. This breath must first recover, gather, and acquire some breadth. Yet what is the point, if one were to keep it to oneself? What sends, sends tasks, and with it, the expenditure of strength, to the point of breath's giving without sparing itself. In other words, the spiritual dimension in which this book abides, and in which it also buoys, is biblical and Christian.

J.-L. Chrétien

Paris, January 2009

Meditation 1

Breath

BEFORE SPEAKING OF BREATH (*souffle*), let us collect ours and therefore take a breath (*haleine*). Let out a deep, long sigh, expelling the air from our lungs, pressing them to their capacity to feel that they are not ample enough for such an undertaking. For it would certainly require inspiration, the impromptu nature of which one cannot rely on. And yet, failing to be inspired, we can always aspire, and sigh again. Let's beware, however, of panting, of rushing the pace and immediately falling into shortness of breath. To begin by panting would be poor form. So, let's inhale, exhale, inhale, exhale, breathe. What is that? What's happening? Let's go on. And above all, let's not hold our breath, and let's not stop our breathing to reflect on what's happening.

It happens that the air comes and goes, in and out, that an incessant rhythmic exchange takes place between outside and inside, interior and exterior, between the intimacy of our chest and the space of the world. It starts with our coming into the world, where we first use breath to cry out in our surprise and incomprehension, and will end at the instant when we will take our last breath, our last sigh, in which we will expire. Breathing is the perpetual refutation of solipsism in action, and of any thesis according to which our life is self-sufficient, or would moreover attempt to be so. At every moment, we depend on the ambient air, and if we can cease eating for a few weeks, or even drinking for a few days, our apnea cannot last for more than a few moments.

Breath is for the ancient Greeks and the Jews of the Bible the very sign of life, and its act of presence. Whoever says "breath" says "spirit" in Hebrew, Greek, and Latin, as well as in languages that, as ours, come from them. The

1

vocabulary of spirit is that of breath and wind. This produces almost comical results, because the word in Greek designating the highest form of existence, spiritual existence, the word "pneumatic" (*pneumatique*), evokes for us only swollen rubber.[1] But the connection between breath and life is also specified in speech: the voice being only a certain ordered use of breath, to speak of breath is to speak of what makes it possible, and in a way to give voice to what forms the constant preface of any speech and song.

Hence the fellowship that poets have with breath. In the first poem of the second part of his *Sonnets to Orpheus*, Rilke addresses himself directly to breath: "Breathe, you, invisible poem!" (*Atmen, du unsichtbares Gedicht!*), before describing admirably this exchange between the world and us. In his at times poetic and scientific meditation of 1865 on sea and wind, in which he seeks to ponder "the tides of the air," its "flux and reflux," Victor Hugo discerns "in the wind" an "intention." He listens to the cosmic voice that never breaks off. "What does the wind say? To whom does it speak? Who is its interlocutor? To what ear does it whisper? Near to the earth, it is sometimes silent; at high altitudes, never. It is the voice. All the other noises cease or stop, its persists. The wandering wind fills the air. It is the great obstinate murmur. Is it a monologue? Is it a reply?" To ask the question is already to answer it, to introduce our short breath into the great wordless conversation of the wind with itself—to breathe with it (*conspirer*). It is upsetting that this word, as dear to Leibniz as the Stoics, has for us been reduced to conspiracies and intrigues. For to conspire (*conspirer*) is to breathe together (*respirer ensemble*), joining breath with everyone else's breath, and to that of the Whole. *Conspirer* names the world's dynamic and rhythmic unity, like the unanimous breathing of a symphony. Saint-John Perse[2] will write *Winds* from such a perspective, celebrating "very great forces growing on all the currents of this world, and which originated from higher than in our songs."

But not all the poets hear the wind with this ear. As men of classical order and sobriety, they do not like the drunkenness of the rapturous ocean, the unpredictable irruption from its breath, the stirring and uplifting agitation of its sudden and fierce mood swings, nor especially its inspiration. Such is the case of Francis Ponge's pages "The Wind!" in *Nouveau nouveau recueil*. It is the wind itself at work speaking in "The Wind!": "the purpose is to deflate

1. In French, the term for tire is *pneu*.

2. Penname for the French poet Alexis Leger (1887–1975), who in 1960 was awarded the Nobel Prize in Literature.

its prestige, to bring it back, to reduce it to almost nothing, to a mean meteor" (in the primary sense of an atmospheric phenomenon). "I know some," Ponge says, "who would praise the wind," before adding further: "They are the verbose, windy ones. They have their weaknesses, these ridiculous ones. They will die down as the wind falls, at the first rain." Yet to accomplish this, Ponge must refuse all this communication and circulation of which we have spoken, and any passage of the breath from the outside to the inside. He defines the wind thusly: "A powerful breath coming from outside man, remaining outside him and things. No interior at all." Ponge's skeptical and desacralizing attitude rejects both romanticism and inspiration, but more than anything, it is the Spirit's freedom that he abhors.

Repeating *Ubi vult* (*"Where it wishes"*), Hugo would refer allusively to one of the most famous statements of Scripture regarding the Spirit's blowing. Christ's turn of phrase in John's Gospel (3:8) concerns spiritual birth, the new birth necessary to enter the kingdom of God, as distinguished from birth according to the flesh. It is this second birth that gives a second breath, and the deepest at that, for it is forever. Let us translate it literally: "The Spirit breathes (*respire*) where it wants to, and its voice you hear, but you do not know where it comes from or where it goes." A question already discussed by St. Augustine is whether Jesus speaks of the breath of the Spirit, or of the earthly wind whose way of appearing he compares to it. In fact, it makes no fundamental difference: in the latter case, it would have to be translated as "the Wind blows where it wishes." The phonetic wordplay of Greek and Latin (*pneuma pneï, spiritus spirat*) must be transposed, which is why we translate it as "The Spirit breathes (*respire*)."

This verse does not comment on what Breath (*le Souffle*) itself is, but rather on how it discloses itself. We witness the visible effects of what remains invisible, and we are not masters of this action's meaning and intention, which does not lie at our disposal. We see what Breath does, we hear the sound of its passing, yet we cannot calculate or foresee it, nor do we anticipate its passage or where it will manifest itself. It is therefore characterized as a free and sovereign power. How, after all, could the very breath that frees be anything but free itself? However precious the act of controlling our breathing may be for calming our agitation and renewing our spirits, we can be master over our breath, but certainly not the Spirit. To want to domesticate the Spirit is already to have denied it as Spirit, and to have lost it. To this sovereign freedom of the Spirit belongs the possibility of violence, that it can bring destruction as well as renewal. Sometimes, in order to erect the new, it is necessary to knock down the old.[3]

This Breath's strong voice does not come to stifle ours, nor to silence us, but to give us another voice and word, one that accords with it. In the story of Pentecost, everything begins with a burst of Breath, a sound from heaven that is "like that of a violent wind" (Acts 2:2). It is not said that there was a wind, but a resonance like that of the wind. That the Holy Spirit (*l'Esprit-Souffle*) blows where he wishes is obviously fundamental: if he invents and improvises his own paths, we can only follow his trace. But does the fact that the Spirit improvises entail that it is only when we ourselves improvise also that we can receive it and conform to it? Looking at it with an evil eye, some Puritan sects regarded it as a serious offense for a preacher to rewrite his sermon, or even to have notes, because they considered this human, all too human, form of preparation or concentration to be tantamount to evading inspiration preemptively. We see an attestation of this in chapter 31 of Walter Scott's beautiful novel *The Heart of Midlothian*. Does not such a conception, however, reverse itself into its complete opposite? Does not the cult of an unfettered spontaneity amount to summoning the Spirit in order to reveal itself here and now? The active Breath, which makes us act, also requires our intelligence and inquiry as one form of its passage. For if the Spirit could not breathe on the one who writes, there would be no Holy Bible. It is true that Christ himself says one should not be anxious about the words one will speak (Matt 10:19), but this does not concern just any words, but the scenes of persecution and martyrdom. The obligation to improvise refutes itself, and does not preserve the full extent of the Breath's domain of freedom.

This freedom is manifested in the Bible, as St. Gregory of Nazianzus, along with many others, notes in one of his *Discourses* (41.14) concerning the great implausibility of prophetic or apostolic vocations from a human point of view. Endued with the Spirit, the inspired man, and so the one who will *become* the man for the situation, the man appropriate for the requirement of the hour and the task, is the one no one could have foreseen to choose, one who according to all appearance is unfit and unwarranted. Such is the foolishness of God, which is wiser than human wisdom, and prefers to be a source for men rather than pretend to direct them in the

3. When speaking of breath (*souffle*) or wind, here in the preceding lines Chrétien means to suggest that we know God through God's own Breath (*Souffle*). Just as we know the wind by experiencing its gust, so we know God through his Spirit, a Breath that, like the wind, blows upon us.

fashion of the sinisterly named "human resources," by which they are already compatibilized and formatted. Yet this entails a consequence of the utmost importance: in the same passage, John's Gospel attributes the same mode of indirect manifestation (mysterious because of its freedom) to the reborn man (Chouraqui translates it boldly: "the native of the breath"[4]) as to Breath itself.

Now, if only a deaf one cannot hear the storm that rages in the world, there are still many other deaf individuals who do not hear the Breath in the voice of the other and his words. Breath, invisible and boundless, passes and acts through human breaths. German has the beautiful word *durchatmen*, at once "take a deep breath" and "blow through." Ignoring the freedom of the One who blows where he wishes, I can remain closed to what is closest, obtuse to what encounters me. Augustine reports in his *Confessions* (II.3.7) that in his adolescence he felt that God remained silent with him, and that by assuming so, he took lightly the words of his mother: "I thought that you were silent, and that she alone spoke, she through whom you were not silent towards me." Whoever is internally asphyxiated, precisely because he is so, does not notice the air circulating around him, and remains in his apnea, when it would suffice for him if he were to open his mouth and nostrils. For the spirit alone receives the Spirit, and breath alone recognizes Breath: we only feed on them, and discern them, when we do not create an obstacle to their circulation. Our pretense of knowing in advance where, and by whom, breath may or may not come to us is a major form of obstruction. It matters little that at the outset we are slightly out of breath, and no longer able to breathe, that we only have brief and puny breaths unable to catch our breath, much less all the Breath that passes by.

The simpler the better, so it suffices to begin with the quick observation that merely in order to utter the word "breath," it is necessary to have taken and received one's own. We cannot enter into the Spirit. Does that mean it is closed? And does this spiritual discerning of the spirit entail a circle of exclusion? No, it shows that the question is badly posed: it is not a question of penetrating the Spirit, but of letting it enter and coming to dwell in us. The Latin hymn to the Holy Spirit, *Veni, sancte Spiritus*, describes it as *Dulcis hospes animae* ("Sweet host of the soul"). It is up to him to come, but it is up to us to unlock the door through him. And not to

---

4. André Chouraqui (1917–2007), prizewinning French-Algerian-Israeli writer, scholar, and politician, who is known for his translations and his commentaries on spiritual works of Judaism, Islam, and Christianity.

then close it again, for what purpose would the Breath's coming into us to transform and strengthen ours serve if it were to remain a prisoner there? Our breath, our voice, our breathing, must manifest in the external world what this indwelling has changed, by this increase in aeration, clearance, and freedom: breath never evades its essence, which is to come and go, to pass, to circulate, and to move itself.

There is another aspect of breath, however, that is singularly ours and till now has been left aside: its tenuousness, its fragility, its precariousness. Some trifle or effort takes our breath away, and one day, this breath will exhale without being able to take one in again. It is said of a dying person that he has only one breath of life left, but when, as in the biblical language, the breath is considered the principle of life in us, we could affirm throughout our whole existence that we have only one breath of life, the only irreplaceable breath of ours. Even in full health, our life is only one breath away. Frequently, the book of Job and the Psalms insist on the fragility of man and his life: it is nothing but a breath, a breath that goes and does not return, *spiritus vadens et non rediens* (Ps 78:39).

Where fragility trembles, irreversibility is also concerned. We cannot catch again the same breath twice, nor can one bring back what Homer called the "winged words" that have escaped from the "cage of the teeth." For better or for worse, these words that our breath has shaped and uttered no longer lie in our power. They fly off without us, even against us, into the souls of others and into time. It is indeed this breath's impermanence that makes it almost nothing, for it could disappear at any moment, and it sculpts the unforgettable words, the horror of insults, as well as the sublimity of promises and vows. The nearly limitless power of speech is born only from breath's fragility: let us therefore be careful not to form a conception of the latter that is only anxious, or already bereaved.

This tenuousness of breath does not apply only to that of man. In the account provided of the theophany of Mount Horeb in chapter 19 of the first book of Kings concerning God's manifestation to the prophet Elijah, tenuousness stages God's true presence. Elijah has withdrawn into a cave, he sees nothing, he only hears, and when there perhaps is something to see, he veils his face with his cloak. The music begins with the *fortissimo* of the hurricane, then that of the earthquake, and finally the passing stream of fire. God instigates them, but he is not himself present directly in them. Then, in a vertiginous *decrescendo*, a *pianissimo* of which there are in the

Bible itself few equivalents, there is the "sound of a light breath"[5] in which God is found. It is in the tiniest of things, in an almost imperceptible simple rustling, that Elijah will have heard that God makes his presence known. Job, who was neither a Jew nor a prophet, said that God's approach and departure were not even noticed. This breeze is sonorous, a light rustling of silence. Elijah did not see anything stir, nor did he feel on his skin this fragile flow of air; he hears it before hearing the words of God addressed to him. This whisper said nothing more except that God, at this moment, was right there—in the tenuousness.

Contemporary exegetes, including the admirable Gerhard von Rad,[6] rightly warn against too sweeping, immediate, and literal of an interpretation that would wrest the story from its context. And of course, in addition to their arguments, let us not forget our point of departure, that the Spirit breathes where it wishes, and thus also as it wishes: this page does not say that God cannot (or will not) manifest himself in the hurricane or the storm. That it arrives in the form of the wind's tenuousness does not mean that it must, otherwise this manifestation would no longer be sovereignly free. It is right to insist on the fact of God's visitation in the breath's whisper of wind, for far from merely being psychologically reassuring or consoling, it contains something deeply troubling, disturbing, disconcerting, because it is not at all what one would expect from the Almighty Lord of being. That God does not cry in our ears like a hurricane entails that we must prick up our ears to the threshold of their possible limits, that God invites us to a particularly acute readiness to discern this divine breath. At bottom, beyond the separation and segmentation of passages that exegesis practices, what is required spiritually when we read the entire Bible is to listen to the bated breath of the whisper, the surge of the hurricane, to listen to the violent wind of the storm, the touch of the breeze, because it is the same Breath (*Souffle*), and the same God, who speaks to us through these various manifestations.

Whatever the writer's intention, let the Spirit who breathed this page continue to breathe into it! John of the Cross will several times provide

5. This phrase in the Jerusalem Bible, "*le son d'un souffle léger*," could also be translated as "gentle whisper," but I have used the literal translation, since doing so preserves the term "breath." The King James Version (1611) famously renders the verse in question as "a still small voice," a formulation followed by La Sainte Bible par Louis Segond (1910), which reads, "*un murmure doux et léger*."

6. Gerhard von Rad (1901–71), Lutheran theologian and Old Testament scholar at the University of Heidelberg.

mystical commentaries on this breath, seeing in its tenuousness one of the highest and most intimate communications of God to the soul. Even his poetry recalls this, *el silbo de los aires amorosos*, "the whistling of loving winds" (*le sifflement des vents amoureux*). This "whistling" (*sifflement*) comes to St. John of the Cross from the Vulgate, which speaks of the small voice (*le léger souffle*) of the Horeb of *sibilus*, whereas the Hebrew and the Greek did not describe the mode of sonority. The *Spiritual Canticle* follows shortly thereafter with *la música callada*, "silent music."[7] For suspended or bated breath remains breath, just as silence is still (or already was) in some cases music. He from whom the words come already speaks without words before speaking, in a presence for which the ear must become divinatory in order to discern. The Spanish composer Federico Mompou will use this expression of St. John of the Cross for a set of solo piano pieces. Estimable as they are, they did not attain the same intensity, and no doubt did not pretend to.[8]

But if breath is the site and agent of an incessant communication, even a communion, between the interior and exterior, between the world and us, as well as between men, by way of the words and the songs that permit us to form it, then when these words become a hymn or prayer, the power and richness of its transmission between men and God does not stop there. The divine breath (or the divine action appearing as the breath, as St. Augustine would say) is mentioned in two essential verses of the Bible, which tradition has often paired together: that which creates man, and that which creates him anew. In each, there is a blowing (*insufflation*), an act of breathing and transmitting of breath. Transmitting the breath is transmitting the power of transmission, communicating the breath, that is, communicating the power of communicating. The first passage, in Genesis 2:7, belongs to the second account of man's creation: God breathes into man the model of earth, breathes into him the breath of life that makes us who we are. The second, in the Gospel of John, forms a pentecost before Pentecost: the resurrected Christ blows on his disciples, transmitting the Holy Spirit to them (John 20:22). It is certainly not my intention here, in a few words, to comment on them theologically, nor to address the difficult questions they raise.

7. Chrétien examines the phenomenon of "silent music" at some length in *Hand to Hand: Listening to the Work of Art*, trans. Stephen E. Lewis (New York: Fordham University Press, 2003), 21–23; 43–48.

8. Constituting four *cuadernos* (released 1959, 1962, 1965, and 1967, respectively), there are twenty-eight in total.

In the biblical commentaries to which he devoted the last part of his life, Paul Claudel delivered admirable meditations on this exchange of breath between God and man, and on the "mouth-to-mouth" resuscitation operation of Genesis. This breath that we originally received from God is something we will ultimately have to return to him in the end, along with all that we will have done, or not have done. For it is not a matter of hoarding a sterile treasure, but of always pondering it more and more, of exchanging it again and again, and in doing so, fructifying and increasing it. Like the spirit, breath is increased by its exchange. The inspired (*insufflé*) must inspire.[9] And here we find the alliance of tenuousness and potency which characterizes breath. In the gift of the Spirit, this invisible and barely audible or sensible breath is the sign of the transmission of power. In his twelfth-century commentary on John, Rupert of Deutz asked whether Christ breathed a great breath on everyone, or had passed in front of each, and concluded that it was not a physical breath, and that he only breathed it as God. The Scripture, however, says clearly that he has breath: for St. Augustine, this physical breath is not in itself the gift of the Spirit, but shows and expresses it. For a long time in the church, there were rites of insufflation for baptism and ordination, in which the celebrant blew on the person (they seem to have fallen into obsolescence). Everything spiritual is also carnal in the religion of the incarnation. Calvin, who is not for nothing the contemporary of Rabelais,[10] says of the Johannine verse with hatred of the Catholics: "For their horned bishops, when they want to ordain priests, boast that by burping on them, they blow the Holy Spirit on them. But reality shows clearly how their stinking breath is different from Jesus Christ's divine breath. For what do they do, except turn horses into asses?" (With what breath, however, are these very sentences pronounced?)

Breath forms the perpetual attestation of our presence and our life. It precedes and prefaces our words, just as it follows them. In silence, I can hear someone's breathing before and after the word, and if we are close, I can even smell his breath. The least anxiety disturbs our breath, which is sometimes its only trace, and any peace deepens and widens it. To approach

9. In using the French *insuffler*, Chrétien is invoking the word's Latin etymology *insufflare* meaning "to blow into," as in the medical act of blowing a gas into a body. In the spiritual context, this captures the idea of God's first breathing life into the vessel of the body, and then later the Holy Ghost. This is all connoted by the French term, whose twofold sense means both "to infuse" and "to inspire."

10. François Rabelais (ca. 1483–1553), French Renaissance writer, humorist, physician, and Greek scholar.

someone, no matter how discreetly, is always to do so with our breath, to breathe. What sustains our breath? What are we exhaling besides expended air when we breathe, or sigh, at the other? What is our breath the breath of? Whether it likes it or not, every breath confesses, and delivers by delivering us. I catch mine, or rather, I take another one, because the one who formed these words has gone without returning. Now it is your turn to breathe in and take inspiration, and to let the tide of yours rise.

Meditation 2

Way

ONE OF THE MOST common and oldest of comparisons is that of human life to a path or a journey.[1] To even note so is banal. But this banality actually conceals within itself a rich profusion of diverse meanings. Our life's path can indeed simply be the whole of its duration: time is expressed by space, and our lived moments by the steps we take. Such is the case in the unforgettable opening of *The Divine Comedy*, *Nel mezzo del cammin di nostra vita* ("Midway upon the journey of our life" [*au milieu du chemin de notre vie*]), where Dante, on the verge of undertaking his journey to the underworld, confided that he had gone astray at that age, having left the "straight path" (*droite voie*): this way (*voie*) designating another meaning of the word "path" (*chemin*). The temporal journey begins at our birth (for the embryo has come to life, but not yet into world's light of day, as it does not yet walk in the time of the world).

But when the young Descartes, opening a book at random, falls upon the striking verse of the late Roman poet Ausonius,[2] *Quod vitae sectabor iter?* ("Which path of life will I follow?" [*Quel chemin de vie suivrai-je?*]), this life path is that of our vocation, beginning with the momentous

1. The term *cheminement* translated here as "journey" could also be translated as "pathway," which captures nicely the fact that, in French, *chemin* can mean both "path" and "way," as well as "road" and "route." I have selected "way" for this chapter's title, rather than "path," simply because it is the broader of the two. There also is the further advantage that this choice underscores a thematic progression in the text, since "way" corresponds to the notion of a "way of the wind" from John 3:8 that Chrétien has discussed in the preceding chapter.

2. Decimus Magnus Ausonius (ca. 310–395), poet and teacher of rhetoric, who for a period was the tutor of the future emperor Gratian.

choice we make of that to which we will dedicate our life, and ending with the accomplishment of this project, with its failure (the path can reach an impasse), or with its abandonment (one takes another path, or ends up wandering). The one who has finished his work, and accomplished his task, has come to terms with his life's path in this sense, even if there still remain many years left to live. In the word's first acceptation, I discover that I am on my way when I've already been underway for a long time, through the development of my awareness of time; in the second acceptation, the choice of path I make, and the first step I take on it, form decisive and unforgettable moments.

Ancients named "Y" the philosophers' letter, for it contains a bifurcation, a crossroads of paths: will I go right or left? If one combines the two senses, it follows that I must choose (even not to choose is a fatal choice), even though I have not chosen to choose, having not chosen to come into the world. As Blaise Pascal said in his famous passage concerning the wager, "It is not voluntary. You are embarked."

Before exploring the several meanings of "way" (*chemin*) in addition to these two, a question arises: *where* are we walking, what for us is this space where we advance? Is not it our home, our country? A central word of the Augustinian conception of humanity, both collective and individual, is *peregrinatio*. The translation of "*pèlerinage*," though exact, nevertheless risks concealing its scope. *Peregrinus* (which has bequeathed "*pèlerin*," and in English, as in German, "pilgrim") is the stranger or foreigner, in particular, the foreigner without status who, as opposed to the resident, is only passing through. For St. Augustine, time is an incessant journey abroad, as we are never more than passers-by or nomads. Even if I never leave my birthplace and rarely leave my house, from the Augustinian perspective, I remain a traveler, a stranger or pilgrim on the earth.[3] The expression derives from the Letter to the Hebrews (11:13), and also the title of a beautiful book by the writer Julien Green.[4]

3. This observation is of no small autobiographical significance. Except for traveling to the seaside town of Dieppe for writing retreats, Chrétien eventually left Paris rarely. After several journeys abroad during his youth (he stayed in England during his high school years, visited Italy and Poland, stayed in Tunisia for a summer vacation in 1983 with his friend Pierre Carrique, and later visited Naples with Jérôme Laurent), he did not leave France after 1987.

4. An American who typically wrote in French, Green (1900–1998) published his novel *Le voyageur sur la terre* (the traveler on earth) in 1927. Born in Paris to American parents, he never became a French citizen, making him the first non-French national to be elected to the Académie Française.

However, even if the beautiful hymn to the Virgin *Salve Regina* employs the word "*exsilium*" to describe our life, this does not mean that we are in "exile" in the strict sense of the word, as if the human soul has fallen here from another luminous world where it would have dwelled beforehand, as certain philosophies and spiritualities (especially the gnostics) think. Or, perhaps it is necessary to say that we are born in exile (*Born in Exile* is the title of George Gissing's very morose 1892 novel). More soberly and less dramatically, one might say that we are foreign born, and that within time we remain so, because our homeland is not a place we have left (or from which our parents or our forefathers have been chased), but a condition *to come*, an unknown country to discover.[5] The hope of eternity has nothing in common with a nostalgia for it: the life we lead according to one or the other is very different.

A homeland is the place where our fathers are found. Where, though, are they? In the cemetery, in a soil their presence renders sacred, or in the eternal life of a heavenly Jerusalem? To think of our temporal journey as a *peregrinatio* is to conceive of it as a voyage whose destination will never be attained within time itself, where until our last breath we will be on route, and whose engine is hope—for eternity unveils itself to temporal beings such as ourselves as something to come. It prevents us from stopping and fixing ourselves in place, as though we could have reached the end. Journeying, then, takes on a radical sense. The book that in English has been read the most after the Bible, John Bunyan's 1678 *The Pilgrim's Progress*, is an allegorical journey based on this tradition. One fine possible definition for idolatry would consist in maintaining that it amounts to believing one has found one's residence, and the end of the road, by staying put and ceasing to travel. To remain sedentary, in this respect, is the false spirituality par excellence. In his opening poem, Bunyan affirms: "This book will make a traveler of thee / If thee desire to be guided by its counsel." Here, the major clash occurs between going and staying, traveling and remaining in the place we believe ourselves to be at home.

---

5. If Chrétien's repeated invocations of the term "stranger" in these passages bring to mind Camus, there is also the less obvious allusion to Heidegger, whose later philosophy's notion of *Unheimlichkeit* is a term denoting what is said to be the felt homesickness of Dasein's mode of existence, in other words, the fact of our not feeling at home in the world. This is stressed as well in *Being and Time*, where Heidegger characterizes Dasein's inauthentic mode of absorption in the world as being one of "falling" (*Verfallen*), a term again with gnostic resonance.

But "way" appears in several oppositions exhibiting its varied meanings. The way can be opposed to another way, or even the absence of one, to wandering. Representing choice as the choice between two ways is universal. In this case, the good and evil paths are distinguished as much by their characteristics as their ends, as in Matthew's Gospel: "Wide is the gate, and broad is the way that leads to destruction, and many there be who go in by it; but narrow is the gate, and straight is the way that leads to Life, and few there be who find it" (7:13–14). There obviously is a chiasm here between the two: the narrow way has the limitless breadth of Life, the broad way, by contrast, the confinement of injustice and death. One is widening, the other shrinking, an infernal cul-de-sac. Even more noteworthy is how *inapparent* the way of Life is. It is not said that there are few who take it and choose to go in by it, but that there are few who "find" it. This decisive word corrects what is abstract and difficult to maintain in the split-path schema: for, in the strict sense, if I must choose between the good and evil paths, for me to enter onto one as if from elsewhere, would imply that I myself was neither good nor evil, in a state of moral neutrality which is radically impossible in existence—for I always already have committed good or evil acts since coming to enjoy discernment (what is called the age of reason).

On the other hand, the one who "finds" the inapparent path, the path that one could pass by without even realizing was there, the one who has exercised his attention and sharpened his desire to find this path of Life, *where* is he? He is not at the path's beginning, but is already on the way! Hope's beautiful lesson: this gate opens when I see that there is a gate and where it leads. Or better still: when I see this gate, I have already crossed through it; I am already in. The love of justice is already justice, St. Augustine said (which, of course, does not dispense with actions, but shows that without this true love, acts themselves will never be just). As for the other way, there is no path that does not lead somewhere, since otherwise it would not be a path, but an illusion of one (the French translation of Heidegger's *Holzwege* [wood paths or forest paths],[6] an expression borrowed from Rilke, as "paths that lead to nowhere," is very unfortunate: they lead to the heart of the forest, there where there have been cuttings, and thus to a place at least partly cleared). It leads to the perfection of injustice where I was already, which is why I do not have to seek a point of entrance to this path. I have instead confirmed my choice of it.

---

6. "*Wege—nichts Werke* (ways—not works)," was the slogan Heidegger gave to describe his collected writings.

Entirely different is the opposition between journeying and wandering, the latter being the steps of the one who is not on a path, but in adventure proceeds forward without knowing where he will end up. Goethe's famous precept from his *Maxims and Reflections* invites us to meditate on this point: *Man geht nie weiter, als wenn man nicht mehr weiss, wohin man geht*—"We never go further than when we do not know where we are going." Among the possible origins of this phrase, Goethe's editor wisely cites an August 1651 exchange between the cardinal of Retz[7] (an awful cardinal, but great writer!) and his friend Pomponne II de Bellièvre, in which, to the question of the first ("Where are we going? [. . .] For whom do we work?") the second responded by citing a statement of Cromwell's: "He once told me that one never rises so high as when one does not know where one is going." To which the cardinal replies that such a "sentiment" to him "seems crazy." As orderly a mind as Goethe cannot prescribe acting without a purpose or rule and going off on adventures in the hope that some opportunity will present itself. That is the maxim of lost debtors and criminals. How, then, to understand Goethe's expression?

What is decisive in it, and what situates it in a different frame of reference entirely, is the *nicht mehr*, the "no longer" (*ne . . . plus*). There is indeed an extra path to the path itself. What does this mean? We begin by following a regulated route, whose course and benefit we foresee, and this very path, as a result of having been followed and having borne its fruit, leads us into a territory where its usefulness is lost, or no longer is sufficient for what it had itself made possible, for the goal we set ourselves at the outset appears too constrictive and petty. And, in this grace of having found, by the path followed, more than what one was looking for, we find ourselves without a map or a plan—unprepared before the opening of new materializing possibilities. We do not have a clear vision of what lies ahead. Here, the path itself leads to blessed wandering. But this wandering (no longer knowing where it will lead) has nothing in common with the initial act of patiently giving oneself up to chance.[8] The examples of this would be innumerable, in both art and science, as well as with spirituality.

If indeed the way at hand leaves no place for freedom or for improvisation, because of the surprise or unexpectedness concerning the encounter

---

7. Jean-François Paul de Gondi (1613–79), French churchman and memoir writer.

8. The fact that the act of wandering can sometimes connote lapsing into a form of straying from the true path is conveyed clearly in the French, as the word for "wandering" (*l'errance*) is close to "error" (*l'erreur*).

of what presents itself, is it a true path according to the spirit nonetheless? Spiritual paths are not railway routes. Bossuet,[9] following after many others, criticized methods in prayer and mysticism (method descends from the Greek *hodos*, which means "way" [*voie*] or "path" [*chemin*]) that are too precise and too meticulous, and that would prescribe, as it were, to God himself his way of acting and manifesting himself. This is not to leave the path, but to follow it to the point where it will be necessary to invent and make it extemporaneously (it is also in this way that it will become truly ours). The English poet W. H. Auden (who, taking the opposite route of the great Henry James, ended up an American citizen) wrote a series of poems entitled *The Quest*, inspired by the Grail legend. We cannot resist the pleasure of translating his humorous verses on the excessively signposted paths, and the erudite knowledge that we take from them. "New addenda are published daily / To the encyclopedia of the Way (*la Voie*) / Linguistic notes and scientific explanations, / And texts for schools with updated spelling and illustrations. / Now everyone knows that the hero must choose the old horse, / Abstain from alcohol and sex" (*The Quest*, XIV, the first title was *The Way* [*La Voie*]). Many trends and books that are to varying degrees commendable, and that present themselves as spiritual, would fall under this irony of Auden's. . . .

Along the route of meaning opened up by Goethe's maxim, it is possible to glimpse an ultimate possibility that truly takes us to another order, that of the leap or the bound. In the West, as in the East, passage to another order is readily expressed by contradiction, by a summons to the impossible. These turns of phrase suggest that the coordinates of the spiritual territory in which we have hitherto found ourselves cease to have any value, that they can no longer detect or locate what is now arising. A clear-cut example intended for meditating on such pathbreaking is the saying from the great seventeenth-century mystical poet who took the pseudonym Angelus Silesius: "Go where you cannot (*Geh hin, wo du nicht kannst*); see where you do not see; listen where nothing sounds or resounds, for it is then that you are where God speaks" (*The Cherubinic*

---

9. Jacques-Bénigne Lignel Bossuet (1627–1704), bishop and theologian who was court preacher to King Louis XIV of France. Considered one of the finest orators of all time, he was renowned for his impressive sermons, the quality of which rank him among the greatest of French stylists. Many theologians and philosophers have viewed his *Discourse on Universal History*, published in 1681, as another *The City of God*. See, for example, Karl Löwith, *Meaning in History: The Theological Implications of the Philosophy of History* (Chicago: University of Chicago Press, 1949), 137–44.

Wanderer, I, 199). The two preceding imperatives are not contradictory. It is a question of seeing the darkness and hearing the silence. The poet accordingly begins with the boldest expression: go where you cannot. How do we reach the unattainable? The Place where we cannot go (simply the Place, which Angelus Silesius identifies in I.205 a little further on with the divine Word [*Verb*], *Ort/Wort*) is at the same time the one towards which no path leads, and which I do not possess the power to advance towards by myself. Sometimes it is when ceasing our looking that we find, and when stopping our walking that we reach the end of the road (*chemin*), for then the end comes. Where I cannot go can itself come to me, over me, into me. Yet that presupposes I have suspended every obstacle to its advent, and that I am not absorbed by the noise of my own steps, nor deafened by the breathlessness of my effort. Because we have paused and collected ourselves, it is then that we leap elsewhere, or that the elsewhere rises up within us. The attentive, open, and available stance, this flexible posture, makes room for a journey's highest possibilities.

The time has now come to examine other dimensions of the way (*chemin*), and its richness of meaning. In the beautiful chapter "Path" (*Camino*) of his book *The Names of Christ*, the Spanish mystic Luis de León[10] begins with a semantic analysis of the term that, as he says, "is understood in multiple ways in Holy Scripture." If its main meaning is to designate "that by which one goes to some place without error," it has four other related meanings. The first is each individual's character and talent, his inclination and his manner of proceeding, what is called in Spanish, as he says, his "style" (*estilo*) and "mood" (*humor*). The second meaning is each's profession, his goal in life, his purpose. The third sense is the work (*obra*) of each one, and the fourth and final meaning is that of precept and law (a very common biblical usage of the word indeed, since to follow God's way is to put his law into practice). In each of these widely diverse meanings, the common core is the regulated orientation towards the goal, the fact of leading to it, or tending towards it.

What matters for current purposes in this simple and clear analysis of the path's cartographic representation is the fact that the way remains external to the one who walks it, and quite distinct from him. In the other first three senses, by contrast, it is obvious that *I* am in an important sense

10. Luis de León (1527–91), Augustinian friar, poet, theologian, and academic. When quoting the passages of León in what follows, Chrétien uses the 1978 French translation by Robert Ricard published in *Etudes augustiniennes*.

following my path. Thus, the present tense of the verb "to be" (*être*) is involved, not the present tense of the verb "to follow" (*suivre*). I am indeed, it is clear, my own way of behaving ("style is the man himself," according to Buffon's[11] famous formula, except that here, it is an issue of the style of existence), I am also my own choice of life and vocation, I am in the last analysis what I do and what I will have done. The law I obey, however, is nothing but arbitrary and tyrannical (Kant's understanding of autonomy is certainly foreign to León).

Without knowing Luis de León, Kierkegaard will strenuously highlight this dimension. If the path no longer is a trace outside of me, can we affirm that two people who do not at all have the same approach follow the same path, albeit in a different way, or must it be said that they do not really follow the same way? It is in the fifth of the "Christian discourses" titled *The Gospel of Sufferings*, themselves forming the third part of the 1847 *Edifying Discourses in Diverse Spirits*, that Kierkegaard asks this question, and answers it clearly. These seven contemplations on paradoxical and sure joys are among the great Danish thinker's masterpieces. At the outset, he asserts his thesis that the path as traced in the world always remains identical, no matter who is walking it. For the spirit, on the contrary, the path cannot be designated in a sensible way; it is a given fact whether or not one follows it; and yet, from another perspective, it becomes so only with the Individual who takes it, for the path lies in the way one advances. We cannot show the path of virtue and say that it lies *over there*; we can only say how we are advancing. He iterates the point a little later: "Thus, for the spirit, it is the way of advancing on life's path that makes the difference, and the difference of path." We find the first sense noted by Luis de León, the "manner of proceeding" (and let us not forget that proceeding means advancing, as one sees in "procession").

This is of supreme importance. The philosophy underlying grammatical categories teaches us to privilege the substantive over the adjective, which is only added, and the verb over the adverb, which only joins it. And yet, spiritually and morally, it is not the same. As the genius of St. Augustine showed, everything hinges on the adverb. How so? The evil will is not that which wants *evil*, just as the good will is not that which wants the *good*, as though we could draw up a list of items in the world that should (or should not) be an object of our will. The bad will is one that wills *evilly*, the good will

---

11. Georges-Louis Leclerc, Comte de Buffon (1707–88), French naturalist, mathematician, cosmologist, and encyclopedist.

one that wills *well*. In Latin, the adverb *bene* or *male* decides everything. It is not gold's splendor that makes the miser, nor children's beauty the pedophile, but rather the perverse way of relating to and desiring them. It is because my will is first twisted and desires evil, that I come to want evil.

Think of St. Paul's remark concerning giving: "Let each one give according to what he has decided in his heart, not grudgingly and of necessity, for God loves a cheerful giver" (*hilarem datorem*, the Latin says in 2 Cor 9:7). To give with a good heart joyfully, even if this joy would not have been spontaneous, even if we would have had to conquer and overcome ourselves in order to attain it, is to give truly, in short, simply to give. For whoever gives reservedly, revealing that it weighs on him and exacts a cost from him, makes us pay dearly in shame, embarrassment, humiliation, and debt by what he gives us, and, in the strict sense, thereby does not give. The gift's joy is what makes it one: the "how" of the gift is not added to it as an afterthought, or as a kind of supplement, but constitutes it as such. This is a perfect illustration of Kierkegaard's thought according to which the path *is* the manner of advance. And, to be sure, it is singular and singularizing: for there are many means and styles of giving cheerfully. Yet the important thing is not to understand this manner as the psychological expression of my already constituted personality. There is the modality of the *acts* I perform, and it is these that form (or deform) me, and make of me the one who I will have been. If the path is my way of advancing, it is just as necessary to highlight the *progress* as it is the *manner*. What does it matter if I am always in a good mood, always smiling, if I give nothing, or nothing worthwhile? Here, inventing our path means inventing our way forward, and therefore inventing ourself.

Finally, there remains to consider what assuredly is the most important utterance of the Gospels regarding the Way (*hodos*), the one where Christ says he is the Way. Let us recall its context. Jesus invites his disciples not to be troubled, saying that he will prepare a place for them, and that he will return to take them to himself. His conclusion provokes a question. "And of where I go, you know the way." Thomas says to him, "Lord, we do not know where you are going. How can we know the way?" Jesus tells him, "I am the Way, the Truth, and the Life. No one comes to the Father except by me" (John 14:5–6). These words, which condense the Christian faith, have occasioned so many profound commentaries that here it is only a question of providing a modest sketch. Nevertheless, the simplest observations are sometimes also the most decisive.

That Christ *is* the Way is wholly unique: as for us, *for each other*, we can accompany and lead someone on a way, and we can give advice and encouragement along it, but we cannot *be* a way, let alone *the* Way. This does not contradict what has just been said by Kierkegaard, for the fact that I am myself the path that I walk entails precisely that it is my own way, and so, even if it can inspire others, it cannot be theirs. A little earlier, in the same gospel, Christ had said: "I am the door. If anyone enters through me, he will be saved" (John 10:9). The statement is as adamant as the one concerning the Way in its affirmation that Christ is the sole Savior. Yet it is less paradoxical, as the earlier proclamation that described Christ as a means of passage and entry to the Father, did so with the term "Way," something designating a place of progression, which implies duration and multiple steps or acts.

If the Way *is* the person of Christ, as Origen says in his *Commentary on John* (VI.19.106), this entails that the way is "living and perceiving." He knows who walks in him, and he acts along the path. Origen draws this same conclusion, as obvious as it is admirable, that the path is self-sufficient unlike any other. There is no need for a walking stick, shoes, coat, or provisions for the road; the route itself provides all that is necessary for progress (I.27.183–85). The way is itself the "viaticum" (*le viatique*) (remember that this word, which signifies provisions for the road, has long designated the Eucharist, what one needs along a lifetime's path). If Christ is the Way, we walk *in* him, we live *in* him, and with his help.

Furthermore, anyone at all familiar with the language of the Bible knows that the verses beginning with *ego eimi*, "I am,"[12] are words in which Christ announces his divinity. Hence the paradox and tension inherent to this phrase when taken as a whole: that God is the Truth and the Life is unsurprising, but how to understand that God is the Way? There are paths to God, yet is not God the terminus of all paths? On multiple occasions, St. Augustine answers that question by considering the dual nature of Christ, both God and man. Through his humanity and flesh, Christ is the Way, by his divinity, he is the Truth and the Life. In his unique person, he is therefore both the way and the goal, or, in the words of St. Augustine, the "way" (*voie*) and the "homeland" (*patrie*). From the Christian perspective, this is undoubtedly true, but some of these statements could be dangerous when misunderstood. There is the danger of performing a

12. Here, Chrétien has in mind this New Testament allusion to Exodus 3:14, in which God declares to Moses, "I AM WHO I AM."

kind of dissection among the three words connected by "and" in the text ("the Way and the Truth and the Life"). Then there is also the danger, owing to our ordinary understandings of paths, of conceiving of the Way as transitive and transitory, as something that can be forgotten and left behind once the destination is reached. This would be to tear the sentence at the tunic's seam (John 19:23–24).

Christ does not say that he will have been the Way, but that he is so *forever*. In his own commentary on John, Rudolf Bultmann does well to observe that these three words are joined inseparably in the "I am." Christ is the Way only insofar as he is the goal, and he is the goal only inasmuch as he is the Way. In the same way, one cannot think that he is the Truth, on the one hand, and the Life, on the other; there is the Truth who is the living Truth, and the Life who is the true and veritable Life that makes true. In eternity, we will only go to be with the Father through Christ. We come to God through God alone.

In any case, to finish with less sublime considerations, this purely transitive character of the way is already essential in the merely human domain. In life, we progress more or less rapidly, and sometimes we stumble, but there is no shortcut. Any student who "crams," as we used to say, knows very well that a month afterwards he forgets what by brief and intensive effort he has learned yet not assimilated. As the journey we have taken, the path by which we reach or achieve something is not just a means that can be erased once the journey is over. It determines the nature of what we will have reached. What I have obtained through a favor or a free-pass has neither the richness nor the savor of what I have attained by my own effort. Certain simple joys, which to some would seem insipid and not especially delightful, become exceptionally intense when the road to them has been long and arduous. We pass by on the way, yet the way itself does not pass, for it perpetually founds the significance of what it leads to.

Meditation 3

Temptation

ALL TERRAIN ERODES, INCLUDING even the steepest slopes, and those of words do not escape this law of time.[1] By dint of passing from one mouth to another (and from one generation to the next), some words are so old and oafish that they end up becoming nothing more than harmless pebbles, completely smooth and round, bland little gossip balls eventually.[2] Such is the pitiful fate of the biblical word "temptation" in today's usage: "Let yourself be tempted," we say when offering another helping of a dish or when suggesting a pleasant outing. The extremely vague association of this pleasure with the transgression of duty, as if coming somehow from a past life or a lost underwater civilization, alone gives the word what remains of its spice. Mass "advertising," which like certain animals feasts only on what is dead and renders what it does all the more insignificant as it gives us the illusion of being original or audacious, has not failed to seize on the term.

Fortunately, we have "test" (*l'épreuve*),[3] the very resilient twin for the word "temptation," still uncorroded despite all the chatter. The following pages will draw upon them concurrently. The universal conviction underlying the vocabulary of trial and temptation in the languages invoked here is that we cannot really know a thing, an animal, another man, even

1. Chrétien's observation that words themselves have their own landscapes is an allusion to the philosophical notion of a "semantic field," that there is a linguistic "territory," as it were, to which a word belongs, a domain from which it derives its use and meaning.

2. The word in the French used here is *bonbon*, the term for a bite-sized chocolate confection.

3. As will become clear, *l'épreuve* can also mean "ordeal," "trial," "proof," or "tribulation."

oneself, as long as we have not been put to the test, which is to say, so long as we have not been subjected to trials, experiences, efforts, and conflicts which alone reveal what we are (or are not) capable of. The Greek word *peirasmos* is the quintessential biblical word for temptation in the spiritual sense, but its root is classic, referring to the testing or trying of something or of oneself. The duality of the French verb "to undergo" (*éprouvé*) where one actively experiences something other than oneself, but also experiences a feeling, is not so apparent in Greek.[4] Yet, be that as it may, to "be proved" (*éprouvé*) is both to have suffered and to be experienced, as with "tried" in English. The Latin *temptare* has these same meanings, as does the German *Versuchung*, which translates the French *tentation* and whose root connotation resounds with the sense of an active search, like a dog following a trail. But Luther also prefers the word *Anfechtung*, which does not have this sense of trial, and refers to a living and agonizing struggle (and can also be translated "tribulation").

The opening line of Henri Michaux's work *Les grandes épreuves de l'esprit*,[5] in which he relates the trial he made of trying various drugs, shows that for him it is not a matter of sampling them as if he were taste-testing, but of trying them out in a form of self-experimentation, so singular was his attempt, or temptation. It aligns with the meanings just mentioned: "I would like to reveal the 'normal,' the misunderstood, the unsuspected, the incredible, the enormously normal. The abnormal has made it known to me." Through the alteration produced by intoxication, Michaux discovers that we are, in our ordinary state, a much richer and more complex mental "computer" than we think. This self-experimentation leads him in the direction of what Emmanuel Levinas forcefully criticizes in the second of his *Four Talmudic Lessons* of 1968, "The Temptation of Temptation." It is a matter "of trying everything, of testing everything," of knowing everything, even evil, which is "perhaps Western man's condition" (this "perhaps" is strange and pregnant with meaning; it is an attempt at thinking, a philosophical attempt at questioning the very philosophical project itself). But Levinas does not take the word "temptation" in a biblical sense here.

And yet, all this still remains vague, because obviously what distinguishes biblical temptation is the fact that we are tested by God or before God, and that the dimension at stake in this test is salvation itself, eternal

---

4. The term *l'éprouvé*, the most common meaning of which is "experience," can also mean "test" or "prove."

5. Henri Michaux (1899–1984), Belgian-born French poet, writer, and painter.

life. It can only be described by posing these questions: Who tries? To what end? What layers within ourselves can temptation uncover? Why can they only be uncovered (if at all) by testing? And finally, last but not least: does what it reveals only come to light having formerly been hidden or latent within us (like Michaux's unsuspected and unrecognized "normal"), or does temptation as a decisive crisis bring to the surface what in us would never have been acted upon without it, whether for good or ill? In this latter case, even the coming of the Savior could be considered temptation, as in this abyssal word of Christ: "If I had not done among them the works that no one has done, they would have no sin; but now they both have seen and hated both me and my Father" (John 15:24). The Good provokes Evil with an otherwise incomparable force. It is not a question here of drawing up a litany of temptations, any more than of studying the many biblical passages that discuss them (along with the traditions that meditate on them), but only of advancing somewhat in these questions, so as perhaps to pose them better.

A key stretch of St. Augustine's *The City of God* (XVI.32) interprets temptation as an interrogation addressed to us, not in word but by deed (*non verbo, sed experimento*), one to which we ourselves will respond with our conduct, good or bad, and that reveals to us unknown aspects of ourselves. To ponder temptation is therefore to question the significance of what is in itself a question, to ask the question of what makes us question ourselves. The beautiful French expression *faire question*[6] is often weakened in its use, having become synonymous with making an issue of something or causing difficulty, of presenting an obscurity or an ambiguity. To define temptation, we must take it in its strongest sense, by emphasizing the *proving*: temptation is a situation, an encounter, or a thought that *makes* us question ourselves, and that dispossesses us of what we habitually believe about ourselves, thereby putting us, even if only for a moment, in a state of vacillation or abeyance, and demanding of us an urgent response in action, which is certainly not so with the verbal questions we are most often asked. I reveal myself in the test (*l'épreuve*), by deciding about myself (or even by deciding not to decide), by becoming who I am, or who I would have been in and through it (it is premature to decide between these two possibilities).

---

6. The expression can mean "ask a question" or "make question," as well as "be an issue" or "prove." In this present context, it means for oneself to be at issue, for oneself to have been put into question, by being placed in a situation where one is confronted with the question of who one is, or will be, in virtue of how one responds to temptation.

Because of this urgency, we could certainly be tempted to say that if the question of what temptation means for us really demands action, to speculate about it would be out of bounds, and a temptation in the form of procrastination. That would be to misunderstand the experimental or experiential character of this question. Understanding and discernment belong primordially to the correct response to temptation, since they are our first act in reply to the question that temptation poses. An essential chiaroscuro in fact bathes the question that will shed light on our selves. That is why temptation is neither primarily nor ultimately a moral matter. Its concept would not require so much scrutiny if there were only temptation to evil and towards evil, and if it were the case that what exposed us to temptation were only our weaknesses, our vices, our frailties (*fragilités*)[7] which are recognized as such. Many men stumble and fall because of what in their own eyes (as in those of others as well) they possessed of the best. Intelligence can make us blind by too much self-confidence (Oedipus, to name but one); power's mastery can lead to impotence and disaster through too much presumption (Napoleon Bonaparte, with the same proviso); moral purity can become allergic and cruel through too much asepsis, and as a result immoral. . . . Conversely, as the unforgettable lesson of St. Paul reminds us, our greatest weakness can be the source of the greatest strength in temptation (2 Cor 12:9). For, according to the word of the Epistle of James (1:2), temptations come in "many kinds," which is why it is impossible to list them. If we take up the definition of temptation suggested just now, there is nothing that at a given moment cannot *put into question* a man: someone who has been victorious amid terrible trials that would have broken others, can crack and collapse under the strain of a simple doubt which to some would have been as light as a feather. Precariousness and poverty expose us to serious temptations, yet security and affluence have theirs also, which are no less serious in their effects.

"Temptation" being a biblical term, can we ask Scripture for calm clarity (something handy or portable, as it were) on the subject? Every Christian regularly, if not daily, pronounces the prayer taught by Christ himself, the "Our Father," whose sixth request, the only one expressed in the form of a negative, is to lead us not into temptation (the verb having been translated in various different ways in modern languages). Similarly,

---

7. The frailty of the human condition is a phenomenon whose various aspects Chrétien treats at length in the last work he published before his death, *Fragilité* (Paris: Editions de Minuit, 2017).

in the Garden of Olives he invites his disciples to watch and pray so as not to enter into temptation (Matt 26:41).[8] But what temptation, and can it be any temptation whatever? Many interpreters, like Joachim Jeremias, believe that this is the great eschatological tribulation, the onslaught of the powers of evil in their final insurrection against the Light. Do we pray never to have to struggle, or instead to receive help with the struggle? But if here temptation names the supreme peril, it is elsewhere taken as a positive. Tertullian bears witness to a tradition that attributed to Christ the saying that "no one can without having been tempted (*neminem intemptatum*) reach the celestial kingdoms" (*On Baptism*, XX.2). We can pray to be tested, as in verse 2 of Psalm 26: *Proba me Domine et tempta me*, "Examine me and prove me, Lord," as we sometimes say in friendship or in love, test me, ask of me what you want. And the Epistle of James twice blesses temptations (1:2 and 1:12), while saying that God tempts no one, but that we are tempted by our own lust (1:13–14).

To which we must add that Jesus himself faced temptation and the tempter (Matt 4:1–11), and that this scene, preceded by the young orator who serves as a model for Lent, forms in a way the prologue in action to his entry into his ministry and the beginning of his preaching. (That he answers the devil only with biblical quotations is the origin of the tradition according to which we should not argue with the tempter, who is always a better sophist than we are. One should not believe oneself stronger than him on this basis: for as soon as one starts to discuss something, one concedes a shred of common ground, by entering into something of a negotiation.) If Christ himself had to face the powers of Evil, could the imitation of Christ, equipped with the strength that only he can give, be without struggle, especially since, so far as we are concerned, such struggle is also a struggle with ourselves? Incidentally, the fathers of the church have tried to classify our own temptations according to these three temptations of Christ.

In order to untangle this complex web of temptation's biblical meanings, tradition has introduced a number of just and valuable distinctions, allowing them to be classified. There are tests that come from God and aim at some higher good, tribulations by which we mature and grow, what Augustine called *tentatio probationis*. And then there are temptations that come from the devil and aim at evil, a maneuver of deception

---

8. The moment in Gethsemane during which the three apostles fall asleep and fail to keep watch and pray is a specific focus of Chrétien's attention elsewhere. See *Hand to Hand*, 64–71.

and seduction (in the strong and primary sense of this term, as that which diverts from the way, and therefore leads astray), what he called *tentatio deceptionis*. There are external temptations that derive from the situations into which we are thrown, those of which we must believe there are none so great that God cannot give us the strength to overcome them (1 Cor 10:13), and there are internal temptations, whereby we are in some way our own tempter as a result of what in us is corrupt and complicit with evil (even the most peaceful and happy life will not escape these). The Epistle of James, right after proclaiming "blessed is the one who endures temptation" (1:12), describes these latter well.

In their explanations of this passage, it is striking to note the extent to which two commentators as distinct in time and temperament as Bede the Venerable[9] and John Calvin agree. In the same lines, from one verse to another, we pass from mention of outward temptation to inward temptation, from a good trial coming from God to a bad one coming from us (or from the devil in us). "Now here," Calvin says with Bede, "we must not doubt that he is speaking of another kind of temptation" different from the external temptations that "are sent to us by God." And as for those temptations born of us, as Calvin asks with a beautiful expression, "what will the sinner gain by searching for some corridor of excuse, saying that he was incited from elsewhere?" But is this leap from one sense of temptation to the other natural, and does it align with the Epistle's logic? An outward temptation, by definition, is only really so if it can at least arouse an internal disturbance.

The internal temptation's inward progression itself has stages. According to St. Gregory the Great's distinctions (*Homilies on the Gospels*, I.XVI.1), distinctions of great importance as guides for directing the conscience, an image or fantasy is presented to me (*suggestio*), I take more or less pleasure in a given instance considering it and playing with it (*delectatio*), I then consent to what it invites of me and act on it (*consensus*). Having turbulent fantasies and troubled dreams is simply the mark of the human condition as it is, and hence guilt itself only occurs, and grows, in the two following stages. All of these distinctions, and more, are put to best use for both directing our lives and for understanding the Bible, which is why it is not a question of negating them as vain. Yet if we place ourselves in the full concreteness of the tried and tested man, their implementation is neither automatic nor simple, since it supposes that a significant portion of the question is already solved.

9. English monk who lived at the monastery of St. Peter until his death in AD 735.

For the trials that come to confront us do not reveal themselves by way of their family tree, nor with an indication of their origin. The devil presents himself as an "angel of light" (2 Cor 11:14), while by contrast the always higher and true God is a "hidden God" (Isa 45:15), who overflows, on all sides, the images and representations we make of him and his modes of action. Woven into the fabric of mundane life, in short, are questions so discreet, tests so humble, that we do not even discern them as questions that God addresses to us. And even the higher virtues have, dare one say it, a backside, a side that we cannot see and by which the tempter approaches and attacks us. We would never have suspected temptation could assail us this way, when we were on guard against what we identify and consider to be our weaknesses. *Corruptio optimi pessima*: the corruption of the best is the worst of all corruptions, says the Latin adage, a fact history and experience illustrate amply. Intellectual rigor, whether it be of a philosophical, moral, political, or religious order, is transformed into fanatical intransigence, the pure concern for justice into cruel iniquity, and the loftiness of the principle that we serve devotionally and with apparent self-effacement (possibly sacrificially so) excuses us from questioning the cause we claim to be serving. This is the tragic truth expressed by Pascal's statement in *Pensées*: "Man never does evil so fully and cheerfully as when he does it out of conscience," that is to say, out of a sense of duty and principle.

In the description, striking like a lightning-flash, of the Last Judgment given in the twenty-fifth chapter of Matthew's Gospel, Christ is said to manifest himself to those who fed him when he was hungry, clothed him when he was naked, or did not do so, none of them noticing, not knowing it was Christ himself who was the poor and humble one. They will have emerged victorious or defeated from the great test without even knowing they were ever dealing with one. It was too mundane to be identified as such. We can be so completely encased and imprisoned within the tightly knit armor of what we hold to be essential or unessential, good or bad, that we no longer have the freedom and flexibility of mind to answer the unforeseen, impromptu questions improvised by God. Like medieval knights flailing about helplessly, falling from their horses like dazed beetles, their greatest vulnerability was their sense of invulnerability. Thus, it is always with fear and trembling that discernment must be exercised over a temptation or a trial's origin.

To this question, however, there is our deed's answer. Resisting an evil temptation, whatever intelligences it has in us, does not leave us as we were, but enhances our strength and vision. Our answer, then, is livelier than the question. The path of righteousness is paved with a thousand victories over unrighteousness. Conversely, fleeing from the question (the trial, task, vocation) does not extinguish God's perseverance in issuing it: consoling is the sign of Jonah, whose sinking to the bottom of the sea will have formed the prophetic figure (of course, this only applies to a fall imbued with acute knowledge of the God from whom one falls, by which he is intensely present to us!).

As for the distinction between outer and inner temptations, there is something porous about it. I respond, by definition, with all that I am to the trials I face in the world, which is how they manifest who I already was, even without my knowing it. The exterior makes my interior appear. Yet that interior is already fully penetrated by our falls and our triumphs, our encounters and our memories, by the whole of the outer life without which interiority would be empty. We can only be tempted by evil because we are "temptable," but perhaps we are only "temptable" because we have been tempted. Milton in *Paradise Lost* invents a troubling dream of Eve, in which Satan circumvents her defenses while she is not on guard in her sleep (Iv, 799ff., and v, 30ff. for the account of the dream): this is what English commentators call "the fall before the Fall," a wounding of her imagination, which will render her capable of a fall, without being an act as such. In less fantastic fashion, other spiritual authors seek, even at the risk of an infinite regress, the secret and imperceptible fault, the intimate slip by which I make myself fragile. Fleeting complacency over a possibility ("What if I . . . ?") may initiate the infinitesimal fissure within me, placing me on a sad countdown to what will be subsequent explosions. A righteous and profound thought can become a disastrous temptation nonetheless, a puritanical (and also neurotic) hypervigilance whereby we scrutinize ourselves endlessly in the anguish that the smallest inner quiver is the sign of damnation, or the very first slide into the abyss. As an expert on the subject such as Amiel[10] wrote, "every trifle is tied by an invisible thread to some catastrophe." Aside from the fact that this type of fear often produces the very thing it dreaded, such self-obsession's insomnia blinds us to the questions that come from the world, others, and God.

10. Henri-Frédéric Amiel (1821–81), born to a Swiss Huguenot family, was a philosopher, poet, and critic known best for his book *Journal Intime*. One of Chrétien's first articles was published on Amiel in 1982, "Amiel et la parole donnée," and was reprinted in *La voix nue*, 143–58.

Are we thrown into foggy ambiguity by all these considerations, no longer knowing what comes from God or the devil, in which case this very meditation on temptation would itself be a fall? For we must not forget that one of Evil's greatest seductions is to fascinate us (even in the horror and anguish we have of it) and, to stun us (in the strict sense), leaving us powerless against its assault. No, it leads to raising the question, the question of the question that is temptation, otherwise. St. Augustine, and St. Gregory the Great after him, lent great weight to a phrase from the book of Job (7:1), which in the Old Latin translation that preceded the Vulgate said that the whole temporal life of man is one temptation, a test. This may seem at first glance to be a very gloomy view of life, but all the stories that have ever been written of the human experience speak of nothing else, being only the stories of our trials, even if their meaning assuredly is understood in different ways. St. Augustine cites this word of Job time and again. As for St. Gregory, in his *Morals on Job* (VIII.6.8), he draws attention to the crucial point concerning the word: human life is not said to *have* or to *present* ordeals, but to *be* a trial. That shifts the problem to the matters of temporality and identity. The great continuous trial that we will have been (for we will in the end be what we will have made of our time, and thus of ourselves) cannot be reduced to any of its moments, even if there are decisive ones.

The Gospel saying (Luke 15:7) that there is more joy in heaven for one sinner who repents than for ninety-nine just people, the liturgical song of Easter evoking the *felix culpa*, the blessed fault that brought us so great a Redeemer, shows that this continuous trial is made up of falls and recoveries in which, through the grace of God, we get up better and stronger than before the fall. Grace that believes amid its trials is not an anesthetic, nor a mere bandage for our wounds, but rather something that gives superior health. Chapter twenty-nine of Origen's treatise *On Prayer* furnishes a vivid and brief illustration of the patristic understanding of temptation's usefulness. Can, however, temptations be reduced to a profitable revelation of what had been hidden in us? That would dissolve the temporal essence of human identity, and make the test a mere lifting of a veil, rather than a site of struggle for the truth of our being. The test's being a surprise is inseparable from the drama of its successful overcoming exceeding any preconceived expectation. A timorous, dull man can in critical circumstances become a hero. And such heroes, returning from terrible situations and suffocating from mundanity, sometimes crumble under the lilliputian attacks of little everyday trials. The weak's strength and the strong's weakness is a commonplace that exhibits many variations. But from a higher observatory in which we would consider ourselves placed by power of our own decree, can we affirm that temptation only manifests unveiled nooks of the soul? Let us say instead, like the philosopher Jules Lequier,[11] who writes these words in capital letters: "Your name is: What you were in the test." For better or for worse, we become ourselves without having chosen the place where we will become so.

This raises a new question. Does everyone have *his* ordeal and *his* temptation, the one towards which he tends secretly as towards the decisive combat from which he will emerge victorious or defeated, just as, for Rilke, everyone bears within himself his own death (this does not mean that everyone dies his own death: one can deprive a man of his own death, which the twentieth century has colossally practiced)? The early church saw the supreme test in the eschatological clash between Good and Evil, of which martyrdom thereafter during times of persecution of the faith (which always remains) will be representative. Those of today's generation, owing to their place in time and the stories of their elders, see the moral and political order's supreme test in one's attitude to Nazism: Would one have been a collaborator, or a resister, or a black-market profiteer? For later generations of the church, however, there appeared the adage that peace has its martyrs also, highlighting that there were other temptations, other struggles, that required no less courage, perseverance, and sacrifice. Existence is critical even when it does not take place in a tumultuous historical moment. If the test is identifying, each has its own test, even if only in the form of the absence of one (temptation's absence is the worst temptation, said Luther following others). Yet we cannot take a divine view from above, nor can we become intoxicated with romanticism by thinking that our trial is maturing within us, waiting for its time.

Great temptations and trials take us by surprise, without warning, and often find us unprepared: by presenting a task that seems impossible, they are of an entirely different sort than the challenges one throws at oneself when engaged in the project of trying to prove oneself. As a little reflection shows, we cannot even in faith adopt God's own view to tribulation. If temptation, as a truly agonic place, constitutes the crisis where I become myself, can we wish it on others? A question such as this bears within itself its own answer,

11. Jules Lequier (1814–62), French philosopher from Brittany. An intensely religious personality plagued with melancholy, he is thought to have died by suicide by swimming out to sea.

evidently negative, yet why? Because this would be to wish for his perdition, because the test is not a means, because we do not know what test would be the place of *his* truth, because we do not have to interfere between God and him, because we cannot draw up, by aerial surveillance, the cartography of the ways of his being. The trial is not a role on the world's stage that we could, even in a dream, envisage to assign. The promise that God does not allow us to be tempted beyond our strength is a faithful word, certainly not an empirical or statistical statement. It can only be said in the hope that he will give us the strength that we certainly lack. The impromptu nature of the question that temptation addresses to us means that most of the time it takes us against the grain, at the very moment when it seems we are not up to it. It is the situation that asks stutterers to speak, the introspective to be organizers, the gentle to be firm, the violent to be gentle. . . .

The ardent and great St. Teresa of Ávila (whom the novelist George Eliot, a Methodist who had become an unbeliever, takes in the preface to her masterpiece *Middlemarch* as the model of the accomplished woman) spoke of the exhausting weight of those small daily stresses and strains, which are not serious in themselves, but which we cannot overcome. Some tiny victories from the world's perspective can cost more suffering and struggle than much more important human acts, where we have placed all our desire for dignity, and our pride too sometimes. It can happen that we are harsh by judging others for temptations that are not ours, and lenient when they are ours, which is unfair. Yet the opposite and equally unjust danger is common also, for we are irritated that others have not paid the price of renunciation and courage that we ourselves have paid in order to overcome what we have, and for which we consider ourselves the living proof that doing so is doable. All the while, other situations escape us.

If temptation is the place of a person's true becoming, as well as of the personal becoming of the truth, then the most fitting word to express it is one uttered first-personally, a retrospective word too (what I was when I became a question for myself), and hence one of confession. Ordeals are recounted, tales always demand tests, real or imaginary. If my name is "the one I will have been in the test," then the test always is somebody's, for it bears a personal coefficient, a unique signature, which will only have been forged in it. This does not mean that we cannot derive temptation's laws, nor think about them, but that these essential structures only reach intuitive fullness in an account that is always that of the unimaginable.

Meditation 4

Attention

It belongs to the highest attention to forget itself, to lose itself, as it were, in what it attends to, as we only pay attention to the act of being attentive precisely when we do not manage to achieve enough of it. For attention to turn back on itself is hence an unnatural act, contrary to the nature of its spontaneous movement, but such is reflection's law, as of phenomenology.[1] Moreover, to reverse itself, this reflection in no way alters its object, unlike when in reflection we come to scrutinize the purity of our heart or some unreturnable gift. And attention indeed constitutes a tension and an effort, the exercise and habit of which we no longer are expressly conscious, but whose acts do not cease to be such nonetheless.

The rich Latin vocabulary of tension and of the verb *tendere*, ancestor of our "tighten" and "stretch" (*tendre*), with its numerous compounds of which St. Augustine made great and subtle use, has evolved with the passing of time and languages, differing in unpredictable ways. *Intendere* and *adtendere* in Latin designate the act of straining, or stretching out to . . . , both expressing attention (like *intendere* in Dante's Italian as well). The first word gave French "to hear" (*entendre*) and "intention" (*intention*) (without a corresponding verb), the second one "to wait" (*attendre*), "wait" (*attente*), and also "attention" (*attention*) (without any corresponding verb

---

1. Referencing the twentieth-century philosophical movement of phenomenology, Chrétien no doubt has in mind one of his French philosophical predecessors, Jean-Paul Sartre, whose magnum opus *Being and Nothingness* opens with a famous analysis of the nature of reflection and self-awareness, arguing that the condition of possibility for all consciousness, including the reflective awareness of oneself in self-consciousness, is a pre-reflective *cogito*.

in contemporary language: we must say "to pay attention" [*faire attention*]). The English verb "to attend" has long since lost its meaning of "waiting," but retains that of assistance and vigilance (think of the doctor or nurse's practical attention to a patient, or of the servant of yesteryear to his master), not to mention the martial meaning of "Stand at attention!" (*garde-à-vous*) for *attention*, as with the Italian *attenti*. But there is a non-Latin vocabulary of "mark" (*marque*), as in the ancient sense of the verb "to notice" ([*remarque*] to be attentive to . . .), as well as the German *aufmerksam* and *Aufmerksamkeit*, the more common word for attention, even if it is a relative latecomer.

A more or less keen attention (or its absence) characterizes all our acts. This is an inexhaustible theme whose history alone would fill a whole volume, so the following pages will limit themselves, in order to clarify the meaning, to two questions: the first being that of the relation between attention and inattention, the second being that of the nature of attention's focus, of what is worthy of it, of what attracts, fixes, or compels it, for which we only have the word "striking" (*remarquable*).

Far from being purely and simply opposed, attention and inattention are in fact interdependent and inseparable, the control of one's attention is nothing other than the control of one's inattention. To sit and fix the mind's gaze, the *acies mentis* of St. Augustine, on something is to turn it away from anything other, and the ability to concentrate on a topic of research or meditation coincides with the ability to withdraw our attention from everything but it, from the thousand circumstances or noises that surround us or inhabit us. Attentive is the one who does not let himself be easily distracted, since he has actively distracted himself, withdrawn himself from what is not his own. We feel physical pain most at night as we lie in bed, precisely because nothing else absorbs us anymore. We might recall, for example, Pascal, who was seized by a toothache and who, according to his niece Marguerite Périer, "decided to apply himself to something which by its great compulsion attracted the spirits to the brain so well that it distracted him from thinking about his illness," which in this case was a mathematical problem. To be unable to concentrate is to be unable to pay attention because one is unable not to notice anything that happens, no matter how small. The legendary distraction of thinkers, exemplified by Plato's famous anecdote (*Theaetetus* 174a) concerning Thales falling into a well while gazing at the sky, and making a servant girl who had nothing better to do laugh, is only the consequence.

Attention and inattention's economy is one of light and of shadow, of patency and of latency: we can imagine everything being equally enshrouded when in a stupor and an obscured state of mind. And yet, if everything is equally clear, there is no attention to anything, for nothing is made salient.[2] To be attentive to everything, then, is not to be truly attentive to anything, a condition from which the anxious person rightly suffers, cycling through a circle of threats in a state of manic attention, and who by doing so fixates on the one thing that is perhaps the worst. That is why there is no other way to attract attention than to divert it from something else by a salient, surprising, seductive, or vivid manifestation. Jaurès,[3] who had powerful charisma, began his speeches in a low voice, so that others had to listen carefully. And everyone knows that illusionists and conjurers, like cheats as well, draw attention to their insignificant gestures with frills, so that the decisive ones alone remain unknown to us. This applies as much to the intellectual sphere, where a book can by various methods conceal exactly what it does, and how it does so. The skillful, clever plagiarist quotes and often criticizes the author he plunders. Traditionally, thinking and writing's courtesy consists as much in providing the reader paths of attention by suppressing the superfluous and ancillary as by saying what one does so as to give the reader a means of control.

But beyond this essential and very general correlation between attention and inattention, which is due to the tension itself, which cannot be equally distributed, as well as with the mental orientation of the mind's gaze, which cannot be panoptic, there are others of a very different and perilous nature. Just as the saying goes, the height of being right can be the cause of being wrong, so too the most extreme attention carries with it the threat of the worst oversights. By definition, attention cannot come to scrutinize what it does without an assortment of expectations concerning what it can find, as well as questions regarding what it will see. Whoever expects nothing sees nothing. Such is the law of all investigation. Ignorance oscillates

---

2. This feature of the interplay between attention and inattention is paralleled in the relation between memory and forgetting. Were one unable to forget anything, and thus always retained an active recollection of the entire past down to the least detail, memory itself would be abolished, for everything would be equally salient in a way that would render it all unavailable. Chrétien discusses this aspect of forgetting as the enabling condition for memory in *The Unforgettable and the Unhoped For*, trans. Jeffrey Bloechl (New York: Fordham University Press, 2002), 56–66.

3. Auguste Marie Joseph Jean Léon Jaurès (1859–1914), influential French socialist leader.

haphazardly between incuriosity and stupefaction. Yet it is always possible that the acuity of our trained gaze, sometimes disciplined over a long period of time, considering this or that type of matter, becomes *preoccupied* in the somewhat outdated sense in which Littré[4] defined it as "the state of a mind too busy with one object to pay attention to another" (Malebranche's *The Search after Truth* has a beautiful chapter on this subject entitled "On the Preoccupation of the Commentators" [II, 2, 6]). No one can believe himself exempt from preoccupation. Take a master of attention and a mind of such immense breadth as the historian of medieval philosophy Étienne Gilson, who, in the sixth edition of his classic work *Thomism*, could "completely retract" his interpretation of St. Thomas's first proof of existence of God by writing: "I have been able to teach, comment on, and interpret the *prima via* (St. Thomas calls his proofs 'ways') for fifty years without noticing, and without anyone pointing out to me, that the word *cause* is entirely absent. This thrice-repeated omission (in the various versions given by St. Thomas) can only be deliberate and must mean something." He saw in it the sign that "historical prejudice can blind the interpreter." Growing specialization has only increased the Lilliputian, obsessive character of the researcher's preoccupations, whose attention's abiding stain and defect is finding, in one way or another, nothing but what it was looking for. We only see what we foresee, a situation in which extreme finesse and the worst crudeness, intelligence and stupidity, overlap.

Thus *Quellenforschung*, the "investigation of sources," which in the past was all the rage in philology, ended up blinding its practitioners to the novelty and meaning of a work and thought, by leading everything back, segment by segment, to what they were supposedly based on. One cuts out a shape to contribute to the jigsaw puzzle, leaving to future generations the remaining pieces whose origin is unknown. The energetic model of attention (which of course fascinated Paul Valéry) sees in it an intense, sustained focus of the gaze on this or that line of meaning in what we observe; it is always fraught with the potential reversal into its opposite, inattention. It is certainly inevitable that attention's finitude is inseparable from chance and peril—as with every finitude. But attention to the precise mode of our attention, and to its blind spots, if it does not deliver us from this finitude, gives it that tremor and restlessness by which attention does not fail in application (in all senses of the word term), and by which,

4. Émile Maximilien Paul Littré (1801–81), French lexicographer and philosopher known for his *Dictionnaire de la langue française*.

knowing itself always less than what it is attentive to, it keeps safe the point of its vigilance. As soon as attention encamps and fortifies itself, it sinks dizzily from the height that it had taken over the thing.

Self-acknowledged finitude, moreover, is its own corrective by way of time. Interpreting what remains fixed, we ourselves change, and there is no one who has not known the experience of reading a book again a few months or years later and seeing new meanings in it, expunging its initial enclosures. Attention's patience is even more effective than its intensity, as it provides the ability to look afresh, without taking up the habits of our old views, and thus to shed our old judgments. If Gilson had not taught Thomism, and had merely contented himself with reading, perhaps it would not have taken him fifty years to realize his error. Nicolas Malebranche, who was undoubtedly one of the great thinkers of attention, meditated deeply on his finitude, as the latter's corrective.

He does so in two magnificent chapters of his 1684 *Treatise on Morals*, where in the work's first part he introduces two virtues he calls "general" or "cardinal," and which do not appear in the traditional lists of ancient and medieval philosophy (I.5 and 6), while our various duties are discussed only in the second part. With a name that he himself dubs "equivocal," he calls them strength and freedom of mind. Malebranche applies to the mind what Genesis 3:19 says of man's present condition, namely that we must by work earn our bread by the sweat of our brow: the soul's bread is the truth that enlightens and nourishes it, of which attention is the work. This word in classical language retained its meaning of pain and arduousness or tiresomeness (*pénibilité*) (it does not mean "intellectual labor" in the sociological sense, which will only appear in the nineteenth century).

"Man," says the *Treatise*, "must work with the mind to attain the life of the mind; this is an absolute necessity." To which he adds: "There is no other way to obtain light and understanding than the work of attention." No truth is revealed to us without attention. It is not enough to have discovered it, however. It is necessary also to preserve it as truth, for which attention is still needed (see *The Search after Truth*, VI.1–2). To support and continue the work of attention, we must have acquired some *strength* of mind, and some authority over our body, in order to impose silence on the senses, imagination, and passions. But this strength is finite, our attention wanes or is interrupted, and there are questions so complex that it cannot unravel them.

The other general virtue, that of *freedom* of mind, is that "by which man always withholds his consent, until he is invincibly led to give it" by the light of evidence. And Malebranche has this admirable (and too little known) comment: "To make use of one's freedom AS MUCH AS ONE CAN is the essential and indispensable precept of Logic and Morality." The strength of mind is increased by its use, through the discipline and patience of our attention, while the freedom prevents us from going where attention's gaze does not lead us or is insufficient. It is the freedom to "suspend or withhold one's consent": an abstention, and an imperative one, for it frees us from being imprisoned in error. "By the use one makes of one's *strength* of mind, one discovers the truth, and by the use one makes of one's *freedom* of mind, one exempts oneself from error." For Malebranche, our whole life and conduct depend on these two virtues. But he does not conceal its rarity or difficulty. They increase through their exercise (Malebranche, who is strongly hostile to Aristotle, is still Aristotelean in this respect), and decline when one does not exercise them. He describes very well fake scholars, whose attention is not strong enough: "Pride extinguishes in them all light; for being always very satisfied with themselves, satiated without a hunger for the truth, they resolve to earn with the sweat of their brow the bread of the soul, a food whose flavor they cannot savor." By positing this strength and freedom as preconditions for both thought and action, Malebranche departs from the Aristotelian distinction between moral and intellectual virtues: there is no area of our life to which attention should not preside, it concerns each of us. Even if we do not share his Cartesianism,[5] we can see from this short overview (which does not exhaust every aspect of his doctrine of attention) that a formidable thought of strength and freedom is at issue. Without attention, it is night, and when it declines, dusk falls.

However, if attention's straining towards a precisely determined goal is what can make it blind in one eye, and strike it inadvertently, should we not reverse the position of the question, and discard the model of concentration, replacing it with one of availability? Is there not an inattention that could be the source of a higher attention? The formula is certainly paradoxical, yet has nothing contradictory about it. We can imagine a sort of steady attention, an equanimous one approximating vigilance, which

---

5. In his Fourth Meditation, Descartes's theory of judgment is one according to which we are always free to suspend belief on matters for which there is insufficient evidence. Because the act of judgment is said to be one of will, he concludes that the true origin of error resides not in the intellect itself, but rather in the will's impermissibly extending itself beyond the domain of what is revealed clearly and distinctly.

would remain more than available, *alert* for anything that may occur and show itself, without expecting anything determinate (neither this nor that), always at the level of our prejudices. Philosophy has above all defined and deepened the concept of attention: has it not, though, been too exclusively concerned with theoretical attention, one that allows the solving of a scientific problem within a clearly delimited and constituted discipline, leaving aside no less precious forms of attentive being?

In a little essay from 1912, "Recommendations to Physicians Practicing Psychoanalysis," Sigmund Freud coined the term "free-floating attention," or more exactly, attention that floats in an equal manner, without directing itself in advance to one item rather than some another. If the patient simply tries to tell everything that comes to mind by avoiding choosing what to say, then the doctor, says Freud, must respond in turn with the same kind of attention, one that does not from the outset attempt to sift between the essential and inessential, the important and ancillary, but rather a slack attention, ever mobile, which expresses well the term "floating" that Fichte had already employed in a stronger sense about imagination. A too concentrated or selective attention, as he says, risks finding only what we already know, or believe ourselves already to know. It is better to take notes in the moment, although this also runs the same danger. This rule has an economic dimension to it for Freud: it allows us to sustain for hours an attention that would quickly exhaust us if it were to be powerfully concentrated.

From a completely different perspective, as we shall see, Simone Weil will criticize the mental attention that often fatigues in vain owing to too much exertion. We listen without wondering what we will retain and accordingly retain more. Reading in this fashion (the author of these lines can vouch for it) sediments the book's content in our mind far more than what we have read for a specific purpose, in which case we retain little more than what we were seeking at the time. (This also bestows the blessing of being able to forget all about it, if it was uninteresting.) If we define attention as concentration, then such attention is certainly inattentive. The question, however, is whether this is the only valid definition. As valuable as the term "free-floating attention" may be, obviously it is shaped and limited by its psychoanalytical context (which implies a very particular orientation of interest), as well as by the theoretical construction attending the notion of listening to one's unconscious, a construction which lends itself to many phenomenological objections.

Yet the contemplative attention we pay to a landscape or to a work of art (when we are not geologists or art historians, which is not to say their attention is not powerfully unveiling) is indeed an equanimous and alert one, because it does not propose to solve a question. The same applies (respecting the difference of domains) to the attention we pay to a friend. We expect nothing but his presence, and take his manifestations as they come. Only the manipulator and seducer have a straightaway calculated attention, just as, in a completely other sense, the friend worried about the health or state of another does. To be sure, in all these cases, questions will come (how could they not?) and different forms of attention along with them, but they will have taken place against the background of this open attention, and of its unwillingness (or at least without any other unwillingness but that the other be the other he is, the Augustinian definition of love). This vigilant, free attention welcomes expectation, the expectation that waits for nothing but the manifestation of what we are attentive to, and which grants it, without rushing, its time and way of unfolding. Respecting a phenomenon's *tempo* is one of attention's vital elements.

Genuine concern for another is not a function of panic or busyness (treating the other like a convalescent is not the best way to make him feel better).[6] It is an attention that acts only from his very presence, if this presence is fully ours. It is a beautiful thing that the word "attention" signifies both openness and dedication—an *unprejudiced devotion* or *unprejudiced thoughtfulness*. What does that mean? Generally, thoughtfulness is understood to mean the act of anticipating another's express desires: as much grace as this involves when it pertains to quotidian and obvious desires (or of ones difficult to specify), so too is it fraught with danger when it deprives the other of having to state them, when, in other words, it deprives the other of his own speech (our good intentions change nothing). This latter possibility presupposes that we presume to know as well as or even better than him what he wants, and furthermore when or how he wants what he does. That is the opposite of friendship, but instead prideful paternalism. Unsolicited thoughtfulness means that the friend is anticipated, that our attention is already open to him without his having to request or compel it, without our having decided what would manifest

6. The use of the French term *solicitude* in this passage, which I have chosen simply to translate as "concern," has a Heideggerian resonance to it. According to Heidegger's terminology of *Being and Time*, our relation to human others, including the attention we give to them, is a matter of "solicitude," whereas our relation to objects and animals is that of "concern."

itself to him, nor in what manner, nor why (and even less so what should manifest itself). For the danger of too much solicitude is that the other ends up feeling like a solicitor, a beggar for attention. A free attention is the one that lets be free, and therefore lets another become free, and sometimes makes ourselves free as a consequence.

This does not pertain just to others, but also to things and thoughts. Attention's laws are not those of our gaze, nor its interest, but the essential dimensions of what is given to be seen. It is the visible that orders our gaze, and hence it is first of all up to our gaze to know how to let itself be conducted by the seen. To construe attention as a luminous ray arbitrarily illuminating sometimes this, sometimes that, is already to profane it. So too is the rule of its intensity: there are some things that desire to be seen in passing, with a furtive or light glance that does not dwell on them (and this is how we see them well, as they are), and others that, on the contrary, call for long and fixed consideration. The vulgarity at the root of pedantry, especially the academic variety, consists in studying everything with the same degree of gravity.

In her short and beautiful "Reflections on the Right Use of School Studies for the Love of God," Simone Weil both echoes and transforms Malebranche's thoughts just mentioned, opening them up to other dimensions. She agrees when she writes that "the formation of the faculty of attention is the true goal and almost the only interest of the studies," or when she affirms that no act of attention will have transpired in vain, even if we have not solved the problem that we have set for ourselves: "If there is really desire, if the object of desire is really light, the desire for light produces light. There is real desire when there is the effort of attention." Malebranche would say that we have increased our strength of mind. But she goes further, and transforms this when she says, "Attention consists in suspending our thought, in leaving it available, empty, and penetrable to the object, in maintaining ourselves close to our thought, but at a lower level that does not touch the various faculties of knowledge we are forced to use." It is not my knowledge that presides over my attention, but my attention, subordinated to the thing itself, that presides over my knowledge, which I use as the case and opportunity dictate, with tact and sensitivity, without being imprisoned and programmed by them. We find again the suspension that for Malebranche defined freedom of mind, but which came somehow at the end of attention's effort, in order to guarantee that I do not acquiesce to anything the latter has not clearly shown me. Here, this suspense is primary (something with which Malebranche would agree, conceiving it as the neutralization of our prejudices), but changes in meaning by being widened and deepened, since now it is a question of putting our whole being at stake: "And above all, thought must be empty, waiting, seeking nothing, but ready to receive in its bare truth the object poised to penetrate it."[7]

This obedience to what manifests itself, vacant and ductile, has nothing "quietist" about it, nor is it reduced to a pure passivity. Freed from any particular occupation that would imprison them, our forces of mind stand ready for anything and everything, only waiting for the light, alert in the strict sense, in the immensity of their exercise. Of course, depending on whether it is the attention of the poet or the painter, the thinker or the scholar, the friend or the speaker, such attention will assume various modes and availabilities, yet it will always exhibit the same essential characteristics of freedom and obedience (let us not forget that there is "listening" [écouter] in "obeying" [obéir]). We are present for whatever comes. And we are there all the more because none of our powers is warped to examine and observe ourselves. What makes a supremely attentive face with this form of attention so beautiful (whatever its features and age) is precisely that it watches, but does not watch itself, does not worry any more at all about its own appearance, for it lays itself bare for the light.

It would, however, be a lack of attention to attention to think that the elevation just described is always morally pure, and that this exhausts its possibilities. For there are sinful, even malignant attentions. Brutal hatred is unleashed blindly, and so often misses its mark. Resentment nevertheless also has its eyes to see and ears to hear; it is well known that envy, humiliation, the desire for revenge, and many other figurations of hatred can sharpen attention and vigilance to an exceptional degree. The modern novel (Balzacian for example), along with life's experience, provides multiple illustrations. And the malicious reader, as Paul Valéry notes somewhere, is a very penetrating reader, from whom no weakness nor any blunder escapes. This is generally the situation with someone who, as the popular expression puts it, "waits to trip us up" (nous attend au tournant) when we are least suspecting. Warlike attention's nature is like this too: immediately discerning the enemy's slightest weakness or flaw, it takes advantage of it with all its power (however paltry) as quickly as possible. Two can play this game, however. We can feign a weakness or oversight, counting on the enemy's

7. Like Plato, for Simone Weil there is a fundamentally erotic dimension to knowledge, which explains the quoted passage's evocative use of sexual imagery.

vigilance. Hence, the multiple tricks that have always been part of warfare (there is the feint of presenting only apparently frail defenses, so that the enemy will rush in to his dismay, or the *simultatio timoris*, the act of feigning fear and disorganization, of which Ceasar speaks several times in *The Gallic Wars*). So let us not sanctify attention as such. Yet with this kind of specialized and particularly oriented form of attention, we return to where we began, to an attention that gains in intensity what it cedes in breadth of focus, and becomes more effective (for it is an attention with an eye to act) by closing itself to anything other than its purpose.

Attention to God, like the expectation of God (about which a few words will suffice here, because other chapters of this book evoke them at leisure under other terms), presents its own essential determinations in comparison to those that have been analyzed. In short, not only does such attention turn towards what is the invisible par excellence, towards the One whom no one can see without dying, and not towards what could be before us by offering itself to our gaze's exploration and the mind's abilities to perceive what they had not yet seen, or seen well. Further still (and this is no less decisive), its temporal structure is quite different. From the abyss of eternity, by its very essence, God's own attention and expectation for us informs ours towards him. To feel God's presence in one way or another is to discover in the same act that this presence was always there without my being aware of it. It is always like what Jacob exclaimed after awakening from his dream: "*Vere Dominus est in isto loco et ego nesciebam*" (Gen 28:16), "Truly, the Lord is in this place, and I, I didn't know." And we ourselves can be this place. The silence we must impose on our inner tumult so that this attention can be possible is one of an open contemplation, one that cannot be of the order of concentration, nor applies itself to problem-solving. Here attention, learning to surrender itself in self-abnegation, lets itself be swept up in one stronger and higher than ours.

Meditation 5

Recollection

In order to need to collect and recover ourselves, we must have scattered, spread out, dispersed. Recollection is an act of unification, a conversion of attention, by which we gather and find ourselves.[1] This act transforms the one who performs it by returning him to himself, making again a center of the one who concentrates. To be able to collect ourselves, however, it is necessary that this dispersion from which we return is not such that it forgets itself, that we are no longer even aware of it, and that we are no longer anything more than the fragments or shards of an irrecoverable form. To notice my distraction and restlessness is already to glimpse on the horizon of my existence, like the dawn glow before sunrise, what might be a center from which to focus and gather myself, and to fix myself by fixing it.

---

1. *Recueillement*, the chapter's French title, is a word that oftentimes is best translated as either "contemplation" or "meditation." I have chosen to translate it as "recollection," where I do, including for the chapter's title, because this is the term that in English conveys the sense in which the particular act of mind frequently of interest to Chrétien is one involving the assembling, gathering together, and collecting of what otherwise would remain fragmented and dispersed. This significance threatens to be obscured, or even lost entirely, if it is rendered as "contemplation" or "meditation." That *recueillement* often connotes something more precise than the English "meditation" or "contemplation" is apparent inasmuch as one can in French always use the words *méditation* or *contemplation*, as Chrétien himself does with the latter, when at one point in this chapter he writes, "*Les mystiques qui ne voient dans le recueillement que la première etape de la contemplation ne prennent en vue cette forme-là.*" Sometimes, however, his use of *recueillement* does designate what we in English mean by "contemplation" or "meditation," in which case I have translated the term accordingly. To ensure the full sense of *recueillement* is retained, when the term "recollection" occurs, the reader should always keep in mind any potentially relevant associations "contemplation" and "meditation" bear in English.

Recollection makes the self move towards itself, the self-dispersed towards the self-collected. It is this tonic movement by which there comes a lively stillness, itself taut, a vibrant arrest of attention and gaze. Yet the athlete does not gather his strength to leap into himself, and this resurrection of attention constituting recollection cannot have as its goal the manner of self-absorption in which I would contemplate nothing but myself, nor the closure of narcissism's impregnable bunker. To what, and for what purpose, do we gather ourselves? And how can we do it? These two questions cannot be separated for an instant, because the way attention gathers what it does cannot be disconnected from what it wants to be attentive to.

Before attempting to answer these questions, it is necessary to gather together some crumbs concerning the word "recollection" (*recueillement*) itself. In its nominal form, it is a late bloomer, a beautiful and somewhat fragile flower from a thousand-year-old land. A Latin and Romanesque flower. In its spiritual sense, the word appears in French only beginning in the middle of the seventeenth century. The language of the Spanish mystics had largely preceded us, with its *recogimiento*, a key term for St. John of the Cross and St. Teresa of Ávila. The word is a twin of *recollection* used to designate certain spiritual exercises, or a religious retreat. Its origin is the Latin verb *colligere*, meaning "to collect" or "to gather." It is an important word for St. Augustine. German has the word *Sammlung*, whose history is wholly different, and for which current English has no strict equivalent. But what is decisive for present purposes is that if the vocabulary of recollection is rich for certain Greek philosophers, and in the language of the church fathers above all, as an essentially Latin term, it is not in its nominal form, but in its verbal or participial form. Augustine and Gregory the Great, and later their followers, do not speak of "recollection," but very often of "recollecting oneself," of being "recollected," or of God "gathering us." That is worth considering: tradition has not conceived recollection as a state, but as an act, or a collection of acts. Recollection's stillness itself becomes produced or contemplated, and to think it is to describe the very acts that generate it, the objects to which it gives access, and the purpose to which it disposes us.

As for this word's fragility that has resounded gloriously from Bossuet to Baudelaire, it is conspicuous by its absence in today's French, where the neutral term "concentration" tends to replace it. In 1839, Lamartine[2] published a collection titled *Poetical Meditations*. This title is paradoxical, for if the recollective act of meditation is essentially one of unification,

---

2. Alphonse Marie Louis de Prat de Lamartine (1790–1869), an author, poet, and statesman involved in the foundation of the Second Republic of France.

then by speaking of it in the plural, is not that to deny it? There are many forms of meditation, however, for there are several areas of human existence where contemplation is demanded of us, and there are, even in each of these domains, a variety of ways to practice it. Even if they are not without interrelation, we can distinguish philosophical, Christian, and poetic meditations from one another.

The first is modeled on Plato's *Phaedo*, his immortal tribute to Socrates, presenting the latter on his last day, during which he dies before dying, by already practicing living the life that is to be in the afterlife. To describe this active collection of the soul by itself, towards itself, and within itself, Plato uses verbs (*syllégō, athroizō*), meaning to gather together, to unite, to condense, to make compact and whole. Withdrawing from everything through which it was dispersed or lost, it is matter of a real self-recovery, the soul's recapturing itself in the unity of a presence and a gaze. This act, both negative and positive, is twofold. The first is that of separation, segregation, liberation, and release; the soul separates and detaches itself from everything sensible and from the body (which is to say, from its absorption in the body). It dies to everything that could make it lose and forget itself in the vertigo of sense experience. Yet this is just the condition for marshalling the act's own power fully, so that it sees the intelligible to which, by virtue of its very being, it is refined and related. The soul frees itself from what fetters it, and becomes free for the task it must complete, one it alone can do: think. Indeed, it is thought's encounter with Being that is in question, and the asceticism whereby we make ourselves present to ourselves only constitutes the propaedeutics for vision. The soul does not collect itself in order to consider itself, but in solitude to see the highest object of its desire, one exceeding itself: the intelligible. It is the love of truth that ultimately collects the soul, and this desire alone provides the strength to assemble, and exercise, all of its power of sight. Gathering itself is neither the soul's object nor its goal. The way inward is the way up.

This dimension of otherness only deepens in Christian spiritual contemplation. Augustine's *Confessions* demonstrate this powerfully. The whole entire work is the history of the author's recollection of the difficult passage from a dispersion lost in multiplicity to an existence gathered in the faith in the unique God. The first and final agent of this recollection is not Augustine, however, but God himself. God alone leads us to God. He alone can give me strength, light, and direction to guide me to him, and transform me along the way. For if I were to try to find God on my own by arranging to meet him myself, it would not be the Lord, but an idol of my imagination or fantom of my pride. That is clear from the first pages, and the first use of the verbe *colligere*, collect (I, III, 3). Evoking the effusion, the outpouring, of God on us, St. Augustine says of this communication of his presence, "you are not brought down, but rather we are uplifted. You are not scattered, for you gather us together." The first page of Book II returns to it in the first-person singular. Addressing himself to the divine sweetness (another important word to the *Confessions*), he writes, "[sweetness] gather me up from the fragments in which I had lost myself for nothing." This certainly in no way means that in this movement man merely is inert putty in God's hands (in which case this collection of self would no more be ours than a puzzle would assemble itself), but instead that the One in whom we collect ourselves is also the One through whom we can recollect ourselves, the acts we perform to this end being under his guidance, and already charged, loved, oriented, and enlivened by him. To access intelligibility's purity, the Platonic soul must first render itself pure (even if the latter is not foreign to it, since it has always already glimpsed it), whereas the faithful Augustinian can only be unified with himself because of God, who, present deep within him, calls to him from before the creation of the world (this does not abolish his freedom, but opens and constitutes it).

This brief synopsis raises two important questions concerning recollection itself. First of all, are there techniques for recollecting oneself, ways and procedures that can be stated and taught? And, secondly, when on this interior path, is it exteriority alone that must be excluded, forgotten, and overcome, or can it play an incentivizing and galvanizing role? With respect to the first question, it is clear empirically and historically that there exist techniques of contemplation just as is the case for concentration. Every spiritual tradition includes numerous pointers and rules for such activity. They are far from useless or senseless. Yet the proud illusion that would launch us onto the quest for self-mastery (where I would be at last the only captain aboard this haunted vessel that is the self) diverts us from contemplation rather than leading us to it. Our time's disturbing fascination with the notion of "spiritual exercises" that are all the rage, and which are more prone to attract practitioners to the mere appearance of spirituality, only confirms the dominion of technique and manipulation. If it belongs to recollection's essence to make us receptive and free, if interior unification is simply the means to dedicate and offer ourselves wholly to something higher than ourselves (or at least to make that possible) instead of being the ultimate goal in itself (which would only be a question of hedonism and of enjoying oneself), we will not attain such heights by psychological techniques of self-will. What is the use of replacing an external preoccupation with an interior one? One hurried distraction for another? In his *Autobiography*, Benjamin Franklin describes his very simple regimen for becoming perfect: he draws up weekly tables, and in each daily column are listed the twelve virtues needed to be acquired or increased (including "tranquility," the minimal form of contemplation), with a note of any shortcomings! Self-examination turns into statistics and charts. We know the ancient story of the king who told his slave: "Remember to forget." On the subject of recollection, St. Teresa of Ávila in her *Interior Castle* (IV.3) writes in the same vein that the desire to think of nothing only encourages and spurs us on to think more. The obsession with freeing myself is just a further form of imprisonment. Only the irresolute draft charts to make decisions, only the old imagine fountains of youth, and nobody thinks more about concentration than those with minds incapable of achieving it. If they searched less, they would find considerably more. No one says it better than St. John of the Cross in *The Ascent of Mount Carmel* (II.4): the act of abandoning one's path is to enter onto the way. For we can only achieve freedom's release if we begin to walk in a manner that is itself liberated. And first and foremost, release means freedom from plans, programs, and measures. Yet, to be sure, this doesn't mean we can't benefit from the experience of others.

This naturally leads us to the second question. Is exteriority alone excluded from recollection? Whether pagan or Christian, much of contemplative literature has emphasized pure interiorization and the need to sever all ties to the world so as to return to oneself, as is still the case today in Michel Henry's philosophy.[3] A powerful Augustinian theme opposes itself to this. We can only pick ourselves up from where we have fallen. And we can only begin to collect ourselves from among the places where we have been scattered. If man has become deafened to the interior voice within him, then, as St. Augustine shows, to rediscover our attentiveness, the exteriority of some other's speech, whether that of the revelation of God in history or the visible voice of natural beauty, are necessary. The recollection that reassembles us can come first and foremost from

3. Michel Henry (1922–2002), French phenomenologist and novelist whose work today is now widely associated with the "theological turn" in phenomenology. Despite their philosophical disagreements, Henry and Chrétien remained close friends. Henry and his wife Anne, herself an accomplished Proust scholar, would often dine with Chrétien in Paris when visiting on trips from their home in Montpellier.

encounters that are unexpected, undeliberate, and not of our choosing. Who is to say what a book gives or reveals? The book I hold in my hands, which is an item in the world, may hold the key that unlocks the door to myself, one hitherto closed or even unknown to myself. And just as we do not beget ourselves, so neither do we possess pure initiative over our spiritual births. In Book VII of his *Confessions*, St. Augustine describes the decisive role that reading works inspired by Plato played in his own development. It was due to this reading, prompted by others, that he was admonished to return to himself and, under God's guidance, to enter the intimate space of his own interiority (VII.10).

In this magnetic chain of books that leads us back to ourselves, many centuries later, there is St. Teresa of Ávila attributing this function to St. Augustine's *Confessions*, which she notes was given to her without her having asked for it. Keen attention, the reader's absorption in what he reads, giving a dignified beauty even to the most ungrateful faces, and forming in the history of painting the iconography of meditation, is not restricted to saints in prayer! As for the gathering power of nature, St. Teresa, in the same chapter of *The Book of Her Life* where she mentions her reading of the *Confessions*, explains well before the modern cult of scenery how during the time when she had struggled with difficulty overcoming distractions, viewing the countryside, the water, or the flowers collected her and served her as a book (this is the great medieval theme of two books, the Bible and created nature). (I remember the story of a cloistered nun who explained that in her monastery, the abbess had installed frosted glass in a window through which a magnificent countryside could be seen. Did the very demanding St. Teresa have such meticulous concerns? And was this view a guilty distraction?).

In this intense contemplation of nature there appears to be, if not a convergence, then at least a resonance, between spiritual and poetic meditation. There are places in the world that restore us to ourselves when we lose and forget ourselves there, just as there are hours in the world whose mute address reopens in us the source of silence, which is the same as song. In his beautiful preface to *Poetical Meditations*, Lamartine places these propitious moments for "inner song" that is poetry in the "yearly twilight" that forms "autumn's end," and the hours that precede the morning's dawn and twilight. This solitude in which everything still sleeps is depicted by him as time snatched from life's worries. Contemplation of this type is the suspension whereby the soul and nature whisper to one another. For there are meditative exchanges. Suddenly, the soul "melts away" with "all that magnificent confidence of firmament and mountains, stars and meadows, wind and trees." Books are not absent, as Lamartine mentions the presence on his table of "dusty and scattered volumes": an old Petrarch, a Virgil, and *The Imitation of Jesus Christ* (in which recollection is an essential theme) marked with his mother's fingers and tears. Yet what characterizes Lamartinian recollection, for better or worse, is its overflow (*trop-plein*), a surfeit of unexpended force. The inert, withdrawn nature of autumn "drives us back into ourselves," but the inner action continues perilously, for this "superfluity of strength" could be converted "into devouring melancholy, despair, and madness" if we didn't come to sing of it.

"Thought's movement," he writes further on, "comes to a halt, like water in an overflowing river, the images, the feelings accumulate, they demand to flow in one form or another." We find again this river analogy, taken in a completely different sense. This profusion and inner unrest are certainly the opposite of the contemplative Christian tradition! But there is still the rediscovery of an unprecedented richness within ourselves that we do not reveal to ourselves, and to which only the lonely withdrawal of the autumn countryside gives us access. As for Baudelairean contemplation present in the eponymous poem and in "Evening Twilight," it is inversely symmetrical: the hour is nightfall, the place the big city, a monstrous cauldron of downfalls, crimes, and sins, where all the faces of human suffering appear successively before our eyes, before being swallowed up. For the poet, it is a matter of pulling himself together and finding himself by retreating from the pandemonium:

> Collect yourself, my soul, at this grave hour,
> and close your ears to the rising howl.

Yet to shut our ears is not to become deaf, nor to forget what would have been heard. Like the theme of our meditation, we take with us what we will have learned there.

Enriched by a new question, let us return now to Christian recollection. In that same preface, Lamartine wrote, "Every man has a wonderful faculty of expansion and concentration, of giving himself up to the world without losing himself, of leaving himself and finding himself in turn."[4] Contemplation for him hence forms two poles of an alternating

---

4. Dilation is a contemplative phenomenon Chrétien explores throughout the chapters of another work, *Spacious Joy: An Essay in Phenomenology and Literature*, trans.

movement: systole and diastole, dilation and contraction, introversion and extroversion. The word "introversion," which dictionaries attribute to the psychological and psychoanalytic vocabulary of the early twentieth century, was first an important word for mysticism. This inward-directed movement known as *introversio* plays a key role in Louis de Blois. The third chapter of his 1553 *A Book of Spiritual Instruction* makes great use of it to describe the synonymous recollection. According to Blois, *introversio* leads to a simplicity of spirit turned towards God, one denuded of all concern for creatures. The question, therefore, is twofold. Do we draw something from the outside world that we lose through meditation's withdrawal? Can we praise a contemplation that does not send us out into the world, and to act in it, stronger and more serious for having collected ourselves?

For, the unity won by a difficult struggle against dispersion, and the fact of finding the sun of justice in the East after having wandered, in no way constitutes a return to a pristine original state. Christian thought, historical and dramatic, never makes an abstraction of time and its ordeals. The risen Christ forever bears the scars of his passion by which Thomas recognized him. And so too it is in every Christian life, whether these scars be of the body or of the heart. The only true recollection is the one that has had to collect itself; it draws its strength and life from what it has had to overcome, and its prize from the price it has paid for it. Recollection, like steel, is forged in tribulation, and as an act, it is not to be confused with any natural placidity. And moreover, the duty to recollect ourselves does not exempt us from charity or from concern with others. Great thinkers of recollection, such as St. Augustine, St. Gregory the Great, and St. Teresa of Ávila, were also men and women with uncommon energy for action. If the Platonic philosopher must descend again into the cave, with its great risks and perils, the contemplative Christian knows that without charity, everything is vain jangling, and swiftly dissipates like smoke, including even the purest contemplation.

It remains to meditate on the decisive question of activity and passivity in recollection, especially since the preceding pages have placed the emphasis on it being an activity. To pose this question is plainly to move on to its properly mystical dimension, where it is God who performs it, and where theology becomes theopathy, to suffer or to suffer God, and no longer to speak of him. Just a brief outline of it is possible here. The orator or philosopher's active, ascetic recollection consists in gathering our

Anne Ashley Davenport (Lanham, MD: Rowman & Littlefield, 2019).

dissipated forces and powers, and concentrating and ordering their application, so that the tip of our attention is as sharply honed as possible. It is hence a matter of both the highest vigilance and operation. The mystics who view recollection as just the first stage of contemplation alone think in terms of this form.

Sometimes, however, it happens that attention becomes so attentive it forgets itself (drifting entirely into what it attends to), and is concentrated around a center that is no longer ours. Being ourselves gathered together and collected by the One we love involves more than making an effort to make him present to us and to turn towards him. The initiative passes over to Love. In the philosophical domain, Plotinus in his *Enneads* (I.4.10) had already emphasized that those who read attentively are no longer aware that they are reading. In St. Francis de Sales's impeccable masterpiece of French language and mysticism, *Treatise on the Love of God* (VI.8), we encounter that replete forgetfulness of recollection which is entirely unlike Lamartinian excess: "The soul, being thus collected within herself in God, or before God, sometimes makes itself so gently attentive to the goodness of her Beloved, that it seems to her that her attention is almost not attention, so simply and delicately is it exercised; as happens in certain rivers, which flow so gently and evenly, that it seems motionless to those who behold them, and those who sail on them do not feel any movement, because they are in no way seen to undulate or float." These are the waters of Shiloah that flow in silence, *cum silentio*, according to the prophet Isaiah (8:6). The act deepens as we forget ourselves and no longer monitor ourselves perform it, but this still is not passivity yet.

For her own part, St. Teresa of Ávila, from whom St. Francis de Sales draws inspiration, abandons the language of tradition that seems to her obscure (is recollection entering into oneself or rising above oneself?) in order to take up her famous analogy of the *Interior Castle* (IV.3). The condition of dispersion is represented by the fact that our powers and faculties lie outside the castle. A first degree of self-recollection consists in turning around and wanting to get in, without being able. Active recollection, the discipline of imagination and intelligence, would reopen the door. Yet it can also happen (and this lies beyond our control) that suddenly we find ourselves inside the castle without knowing how we entered, nor from where, and without having even been conscious of entering. It is the discreet call from the Shepherd and Supreme Host of the castle's doing. All we experienced, St. Teresa says, was a "sweet contraction" (*encogimiento*).

This contemplation is where God alone seeks and finds us. Still, we had to let ourselves be found.

For this, we need to be ourselves in person somewhere, rather than in a thousand rotating places under various masks. Recollection is an act of presence: to oneself, certainly, but even more so, a presence of self that can reach, join, touch, seize. Many suffer from the fact that they think nothing ever happens to them. But what if they weren't there when it did? To attain this ability to be present supposes the opposite of stiffness and withdrawal: a flexibility, a pliability, a letting go, and, to put it bluntly, an exposure and a nakedness, such that what comes to meet us has permission to do so without detours, and without having to cross multiple lines of fortification. What could be more nude and receptive than an attentive, collected face? If mysticism's high summits may seem far from us, the fact remains that with the smallest act of contemplation and attention, the target on our heart begins to be traced where the essential can come to pierce us.

Meditation 6

Blessing

THERE ARE SOME LANGUAGES in which two members of a relationship have the same name, despite the great difference of their acts. Hence in French, for example, the one who receives and the one who is received are both called "hosts" (*hôtes*), while English distinguishes "host" and "guest." The mutuality of the name, by which I am the host of my host, enshrines in the light of language the essence of hospitality. There is in fact no opposition between activity and passivity, for whoever receives at home also receives in return, not something, but someone, and so the grace of the guest's presence. And just as there's an art to being received, so too then there's an art to receiving.

In the biblical languages, Hebrew and Greek, just as in Latin and French, the first blessing of the word "blessing" (*bénédiction*) is that we can use it just as well for that which comes from God to man as for what comes from man to God. Such is not the case in German, which uses distinct verbs, for instance. Now, these two acts obviously differ (much more than with hospitality), since the man who blesses God thanks, praises, recognizes, and sings to him, but does not render God any better off, nor bestow any new feature to God, even if doing so allows God's glory to shine within him and to become a site of passage and of transit. Conversely, as the great Origen noted in his commentary on the Epistle to the Romans (IX.14), God's blessing for man always confers a gift that transforms us, perhaps for ever. Under the extraordinary diversity of its guises (whether by song, poetry, or cry), in praise and stammering, blessing assumes human speech's highest possibility, the incandescence of *Yes*. There is the silent blessing too, one nonetheless pregnant with words, of hands that care, lift, soothe, or kiss, and whose gestures say yes.

So vast is blessing's spaciousness that a few pages cannot in any way do to cover it. What follows will concentrate on just one of its paradoxical and decisive forms: the blessing *wrested* at the insistence of one who asks for it in both good and bad times. We will start with a famous scene, the twelfth and final chapter of Book III of St. Augustine's *Confessions*, before going back to its biblical sources and exploring the tradition they established. Deeply troubled by her son's errant thought and deeds, Augustine's mother, Monica, does not cease from crying while praying, and from praying while weeping, begging God to grant grace to the one whom tradition will come to nickname the Doctor of Grace. As St. Augustine says with the force of the biblical sense of the word, the "ears" of God were near to his mother's heart, and God sends her a dream as a first sign of hope. However, this is not enough for Monica, so immense is her anguish over a son whom she considers spiritually "dead"; her tears plead for nothing else than for his resurrection, this rebirth of the soul that is conversion, which St. Augustine himself would later reflect on. Through the mouth of a bishop whom she goes to consult, she will obtain a second "response" from God. Yet how?

She requests the bishop confer with her son to discuss and free him from his Manichaean errors. The bishop, who back in the prime of his youth had himself been close to Manichaeism, is not at all in favor of the intervention she calls for; he thinks that Augustine's intelligence will eventually be able to see for itself the untenable nature of this tragic and dualistic religion (along with its complex mythology) that holds the body and the world, and the gift of life that brings us into it, in abhorrence. Father Jean-Nicolas Grou, the eighteenth-century Jesuit mystic, and also the remarkable translator of Plato's dialogues, published *Morale tirée des Confessions de Saint Augustin* in 1786, wherein he emphasizes, regarding this scene in question, that when it comes to faith, it is more crucial and precious to pray for his children than to give them moral lectures, as "reproaches often contain sharpness and bitterness"—which, as everyone knows, typically produce the opposite outcome of what they had intended, and have the added self-serving benefit of justifying and reinforcing our own bitterness. For such an attitude, there's no such thing as too small a win, and being right is always considered a good thing. As Father Grou says, it is rather by prayer, and not reprimands, that we can become for a second time (in another order) father or mother to our children.

In any event, Monica was unsatisfied with the bishop's response, and, crying and beseeching, she insists on not letting him go until, "impatient with tedium" and the fatigue (*taedio*) she has caused him, having had enough and being unable to take it anymore, he tells her to go away, assuring her, "it is not possible that the son of so many tears should perish." Monica takes this response as one coming from God himself, "as if it has resounded from heaven," and these are that Book's final words. A learned commentator, O'Donnell,[1] avers that in these lines Augustine does not portray his mother in a flattering light. Is that the case? How could there be a shameful subtext in what appeared to him as the intercession that decided, by the grace of God, his own salvation? For, he was not the son of his mother's prayerful tears, but would become so by becoming a son of God through adoption in baptism. How could Monica's unwelcome pleading, which alone earned her this admirable blessing, be even implicitly condemned? The bishop certainly blessed her, pronouncing a blessing on her son, because he had had enough and wished that she would finally let him alone, yet the story very much presents this blessing as coming from God himself, as a "response" from God. Monica does not give up on her desire, her desire for life for her son. This is a very plain example of a benediction wrested through insistence.

This lesson of insistence is a great biblical one. It dates back to the patriarchs themselves. In the deeply moving eighteenth chapter of Genesis (vv. 17–33) when God declares to Abraham his intention to smite Sodom and Gomorrah's wickedness, Abraham himself insists (albeit in humble and reverential words) on bargaining and negotiating at length with the Lord. If there are fifty righteous people in the city, should we not spare it? And forty-five? And forty? And thirty? And twenty? And what if there are just ten? This story lying at the origin of the Jewish tradition's viewing the righteous as pillars of the world, is obviously also a lesson on prayer. Above all, though, in Genesis there is Jacob's struggle with the angel, during which, when the latter asks the former to let him go, Jacob replies, "I will not let you go, unless you bless me" (32:26), and obtains so deep a blessing that it changes his name from Jacob to Israel. Here, insistence is not restricted to words alone, but involves an agonic intimacy of the hand to hand.[2]

---

1. James J. O'Donnell (1950–), an American classicist. See *Augustine: A New Biography* (London: HarperCollins, 2005).

2. For another discussion of this biblical scene, see also *Hand to Hand*, 1–17.

And what struggle could be more a matter of life and death than the one for a blessing? We would place very little stock in it, and would make very little of it, if we did not think that such struggling deserves all of our strength, including those unknown reserves which open up when we no longer have any strength except that of not letting go, of not yielding, and of emptying ourselves so as to ensure that the efforts we have already expended, of our own doing, will not have been spent for nothing. We must rely on the inertial force of great desires that continue on once they are begun, and desire in and for us, even when it seems (from our own limited perspective) that we no longer have the resources still to desire. In the violent battle for the benediction, we are our own worst enemy; our adversary is not the one who can deny us the blessing but that within us that would discourage us from continuing to ask for it. Just as there are holy angers, so is there not also holy impudence, a justifiable absence of shame and restraint to ask for the *Yes*, if it is that of life itself and for life itself? That is the thought on which we must meditate.

Luke's Gospel relates two parables specifically concerning the insistence of the request that do not appear in the other Synoptic Gospels. They are a recurrent source of inspiration and fortitude in the Christian tradition of prayer. The first (11:5–8) is found in a context that throws in relief its exceptional importance. It appears, in fact, between Jesus's teaching to his disciples of the Christian prayer par excellence (the "Our Father") and the general precepts concerning the act of prayer, which themselves have parallels in Matthew ("Ask, and it will be given you; seek, and you shall find; knock, and it shall be opened unto you"). This parable, thus, lies at the center of prayer's deepening progression: how and why it asks for (and obtains) what it does. What is the parable's teaching? A man receives in the middle of the night an impromptu visit from a friend who is on a trip, and doesn't have anything at home to feed him. He knocks on the door of his nearby friend's place, asking for three bread loaves. This inconvenient request bothers the friend, who replies, "Do not trouble me; the door is now shut, and my children and I are in bed; I cannot rise and give to you." We certainly have no need of the Bible to know this sort of reply, an excuse based on everyday reasons, for we have all heard and said similar things. We would be happy to do it in other circumstances, but this is not the time, or that we do not have the time. Christ straightforwardly states the story's lesson: "I say unto you, though he will not rise and give him because he is his friend, yet because of his importunity (*anaideian*) he will

57

rise and give him as many as he needs." The story involves an unmistakably suggestive ellipsis, signaled by the key word "importunity": the one who knocks is not content with this refusal, not offended by this rebuff, and continues to insist until the door is opened to him. Most of us would doubtless have left with a curse on our lips or in our heart, complaining to our guest about the bad will, laziness, and selfishness of the man we had till then taken for a friend. . . .

The church fathers have offered beautiful and subtle allegorical interpretations of the "three loaves," even down to the detail of the fact that the unexpected visitor comes "from the way" (which is translated as "journey"). And yet, whatever their focuses and merits, these interpretations divert us from what in this case is the essential. In chapter 18 (vv. 1–8), Luke again presents a parable about the necessity of "praying without ceasing and not to faint." An unjust judge refuses to do right by a widow who requests his help. "But afterward he said within himself, 'Though I fear not God, nor regard man; Yet because this widow troubles me, I will avenge her, lest by her continual coming she weary me.'" These parables invite us to do what Monica did for her son. She has, as used to be said (the dictionary[3] provides several examples from classical theater), "wearied him with her prayers" and tears until he delivers, not bread or justice, but his response and his blessing. She has used her patience and resilience. The Latin word *taedium*, boredom, weariness, fatigue, which St. Augustine uses to describe the bishop's mood, is the same one he uses in his *Questions on the Gospels* (II.21) to describe the reluctant friend in Luke's first parable, who finally gives the loaves, "not out of friendship, but compelled by weariness" (*taedio compulsus*). Monica's demeanor is not portrayed in a negative light, then, as if she were a quarrelsome and terribly rude woman, but in the Gospel's light.

The evangelical parables describing God's behavior towards mankind, and here, the granting of prayer (the gift of blessing), are both assuredly paradoxical (and are not the only ones to be so). Jesus invites us to comport ourselves in prayer to God as did the characters of these stories towards the friend who does not want to be bothered and the judge who does not want to render justice. Well before the Neoplatonist Proclus applied such a distinction to the symbolism of Greek myths, St. Augustine in these same *Questions* (II.45) distinguishes between the parables "according to

---

3. In the French, here Chrétien refers to the *Littré*, the eponymous French dictionary compiled by Émile Maximilien Paul Littré (1801–81).

resemblance" and those that start "from dissimilarity as such" (the difference between God's and our human character suggested by the story). The parables of dissimilarity, through their narrative structure, compare God to some little disreputable man, deploying a logic of surplus (*surcroît*) and excess: if you end up winning solicitation's war of attrition and overcoming the resistance of evil and ungenerous men, this is all the more reason to invite you not to relinquish your own desire before the just and merciful God. "If you then, being evil, know how to give good gifts to your children, how much more (*quanto magis*) shall your heavenly Father give the Holy Spirit to them who ask him!" (11:13). To give the Holy Spirit is not to provide a blessing, but the very source of every blessing, the power of movement, of circulation, of communication, of benediction itself.

By the grace of God, this lesson does not fall on deaf ears! Monica understands it well, and it is the intercession of her tears and her struggle to obtain the blessing that he becomes no longer Augustine, but St. Augustine. As one of the great figures of early Western monasticism, so St. John Cassian also praises persistence (*importunitas*), importunity in prayer, referring to the Gospel of Luke. In his *Conferences* (IX.34), speaking in the name of those who believe themselves to be devoid of any great virtue, he has monk Isaac say, "But with importunity, which the Lord promises is within reach of whoever desires it, can we not have everything that we will ask of him according to is will? Let us stop hesitating, which would betray a lack of faith, and let us persist in prayer! [. . .] In his desire to grant us heavenly and eternal goods, the Lord himself urges us to constrain him, as it were, by our importunity. And far from rejecting the importunate with contempt, he encourages and praises them."[4] The meaning of the word *importun* repeated several times wavers. What would be importune for us, as humans, is not so for God.

Importunity, which here amounts to the entreaty's insistence and firmness, will obtain the blessing it seeks, because it is already itself a blessing and a grace. It does not, in short, derive from our good deed nor our awareness of our perceived merits, but from God's promise, and the effort with which we seize and adhere to it. For John Cassian, hesitation in asking reveals unfaithfulness; it is not the mark of a refined and delicate soul, but the birth of doubt. For in the life-or-death struggle to obtain the

4. The quoted Cassian passage has been rendered literally into English from the French of Eugène Pichery's 1959 Cerf edition on which Chrétien here relies, and thus differs stylistically from the 1894 C. S. Gibson English standard translation that will be familiar to some readers.

blessing, it is not a matter of being delicate. Ordinary politeness is inappropriate with the Lord of being. As with self-doubt, such is not the time to cultivate and exercise worry, nor is it a moment to abolish or struggle against assurance, because that is the point of departure for the very asking, and something acquired once and for all. One cannot bless oneself, and the blessing that we ask from God puts in play a dimension that, by definition, we ourselves cannot hoist ourselves up to.

Jean-Joseph Surin, a great seventeenth-century Jesuit mystic, who journeyed through many terrible melancholic nights, in his *Questions sur l'amour de Dieu* (II.4), recounts in his own words the same thing as John Cassian, referring as well to the Gospel of Luke: "Only through the life of faith do we snatch treasures from God's hands," treasures of blessing. That same century, Bossuet repeats the vocabulary of importunity in one of his greatest masterpieces, *Meditations on the Gospel*. He sees a gradation of belief among asking, seeking, and knocking: "Persevere in knocking, to the point of making yourself unwelcome (*importun*), if you can. There is a way to force God, and to wrest his graces from him: and that way is to ask relentlessly with firm faith [. . .]. And although God seems not to hear us, or even repels us, we must always keep knocking." Bossuet adds further on: "The importunity that is necessary for God's help is the urgency that was spoken of above." The word is found once more, albeit with a tone of its own, under the pen of St. Thérèsa of Lisieux, who, in a letter to her aunt from November 18, 1889, writes, "Alas! I am so flawed that my poor prayers are doubtless worthless, but there are beggars who by dint of importuning obtain their desires; I will do as they do, and the good Lord will be unable to send me away empty-handed." From century to century, the common thread of Luke's parables therefore runs through the words of prayer.

Such words are the complete antithesis of quietism: it is not a question of aiming for a state of flexible indifference and detachment in which we would let ourselves be carried away by the gusts of Providence, but, as Bossuet insists (and for good reason) of acting, by knocking, and knocking still again. The prayerful, ultimately for their greater good, evince none of the tragic reticence and politeness of Franz Kafka's famous parable, whose character spends his entire life before the door of the Law, questioning and bribing the doorkeeper without ever gaining admittance, before learning just prior to his death that this door was only for him.[5] As Kierkegaard himself will say, prayer is a struggle. But how is that to be understood correctly?

5. See Kafka, *The Trial*, trans. Breon Mitchell (New York: Schocken, 1998), 217–24.

In turn, two questions arise. In his 1855 novel *The Newcomes*, the English author W. M. Thackeray wrote that rude, selfish, pushy people get what they want typically, at least in daily life, because we want peace and wish to avoid conflicts, and so, while inwardly grumbling over them, we eventually give in. Does this apply to spiritual matters as well? An enigmatic saying of Christ in Matthew's Gospel (11:12) recounts that since John the Baptist, "the kingdom of heaven suffers violence, and the violent take it by force" (Flannery O'Connor made the latter phrase the title of one of her beautiful novels). In the twelfth century, Rupert of Deutz affirmed that because with Christ the kingdom has drawn near, we can seize it by hand, and that such violence belongs to penitent sinners (*On Matthew*, IX). Seeking to wrest a divine benediction, the violence of prayer is the violence of uncloaked desire. What does this mean?

Such insistence in no way resembles that of a litigant or a lawyer, for this mode of petition is not based on an argument that would explain (with good or bad reasons) how it is justified, by whom it must be satisfied, and what names we have to classify it. The friend asks for bread, the widow for justice. But if they continue to do so even once they have been refused, it is precisely because the arguments have not been received and heard, and repeating them would do nothing. Thus, they persist in declaring that they desire, that this desire lives on, that they will not go away, not even with an expression of offended dignity. Whoever confesses his desire exposes himself, reveals himself, strips himself bare, and, by doing so, offers himself up to be taken, which is why, with human humor, we most often cloak our own desires, and all the more so when they are important to us, as Marcel Proust describes admirably, in a thousand ways, in *In Search of Lost Time*. The weakness of naked desire's expression, though, is also a strength in a higher sense, provided that it maintains the shock of its irruption, and provided that it does not conceal itself immediately with the first rags that come along after it is rebuffed or met with derision. For true speech can only increase, deepen, and resound through speech itself, and this applies to desire's word. And time's apprenticeship, according to the human law of desire's nudity, is what makes man properly human—without end. A desire that was either satisfied or renounced at the first delay or rebuff (and thereby revealed that it was only caprice) would only reveal the work of death in us.

Throughout his work, St. Augustine reflects on how God's delays are responses to us that open the space for maturation and growth, reinforcing desire. Time shapes desire as we forge steel. And what God teaches us by not satisfying us, when the petition is just, isn't that we ask too much, and that we should lessen our demands, but that we either are not yet pleading enough or that God is dilating us so that we may receive what is being prepared for us. Such is St. Augustine's lesson. A desire that was not brazen, which is to say, naked in announcing itself, would be an act of deception and hence manipulation. In any event, it would certainly not expand.

A second, final question must be addressed. By naively and irrationally affirming desire's omnipotence, would not this call of insistence, importunity, and boldness, with its eye to wresting God's benediction, amount to what the English call "wishful thinking," thereby transforming us into children? Let's revisit Monica. The two "responses" that her prayerful tears receive from God (the dream and the word of blessing extracted from the bishop) were for her signs for hopeful confidence. There was no miracle that then changed, converted, or awoke Augustine. Everything remains as it was. He was spiritually dead, and so he remained for a long while afterwards. She continued to pray through desire itself, more firmly and less anxiously, yet with no less concern. She extracted a blessing, rather than extorting a miracle. The story, therefore, is neither puerile nor immediate (two terms that are ultimately identical).

We never cease requesting finite things unconditionally, which is to say, conditioning and conditioned, we ourselves break, and we ourselves die in one manner or other (there are many), by renouncing what was unconditional in our field of desire. Yet unconditional desire alone can and must be unconditional. And only the desire of life, of Life, can be so, for such unconditionality already belongs to life itself, which is its first action. Here we reach our conclusion: the desire for a blessing is already itself one, and that is why nothing can resist it. The desire for God, all tradition shows, is already a form of his presence and approach. Who, after all, but he would be able to enkindle it?

As for the friend and the widow of Luke's parables, they asked only for their due, by pleading in their different ways for the friend to be a friend, and for the judge to be just. Their importunity's success is not solely to have obtained what they desired for themselves—it is also to have accomplished an act of justice through the judge (even if this was not out of the love of justice), and to have brought about an act of friendship through the friend (even if this was not by friendship). Who knows what may come of it? For, having gotten the other to do the right thing, their impertinence will have been, in its own way, a blessing.

Meditation 7

Peace

DOES NOT THE BEAUTIFUL name of peace designate, at bottom, an absence, one wholly intermittent, namely that of war's absence, and hence merely its cessation? Is not peace always a respite, a truce? We still term the two decades between the two World Wars the inter-war period: this expression applies solely to Europe and to armed conflicts between states, for these years saw the end of Ireland's struggle for dignity and independence, a complex and improvident achievement that left a difficult inheritance, and the terrible Spanish Civil War, ruthless like every civil war, and a training ground for some of the powers that were eventually to confront each other. The few exceptional decades of peace following the 1915 Congress of Vienna up to the Crimean War contained social conflicts and revolutions, colonial wars across the rest of the world, along with the era inaugurated by the Second World War's Yalta Conference that will remain known to history as the "Cold War," and of course, the arms race. Far from the interwar period designating a specific one, is it not the essence of what with history we call peace?

But if man wages war, or prepares for the next one, by meditating on or brooding over the one before, shouldn't our doubts about peace go further, until we come to view it as an illusion or fantasy? One such doubt is old and recurring. A word from the prophet Jeremiah (6:14) speaks of those who say, "Peace! Peace!" when there is no peace. Yet Jeremiah is thinking only of a particular period, while Clinias, one of the interlocutors in Plato's last dialogue the *Laws* (his at once majestic and meticulous, strange philosophical testament), which takes the exceedingly slow course of a mighty river, for his part, says: "For what most of the people call

63

peace is so in name only, while in fact all the cities are, by nature, always involved in undeclared (*akèrykton*) warfare against all other cities."[1] This Greek word also has the connotation of "implacability." Ancient Greece, which bequeathed us the admirable and fragile heritages of philosophy and democracy (two distinct legacies, as it happens), also invented what Anglophone historians term the "Western model of warfare," that of the pitched and decisive battle, concentrating the maximum amount of violence in the minimum amount of time and space (in order to finish it), which terrified other civilizations (which isn't to say that they were themselves peaceful, but simply that they fought differently).

Of Europe's balance of power (which later became the balance of terror in the era of nuclear weapons, and which Kant had already said could not be a basis for peace, since nothing could break it), Montesquieu, in *The Spirit of the Laws* (XII.17), wrote, "Each monarch keeps as many armies on foot as if his people were in danger of being destroyed; and we call peace this state of war of all against all." The subtle and delicate Emily Dickinson, one of American poetry's greatest voices, goes so far to speak here of "fiction." "Peace is a fiction of our faith." And elsewhere: "I many times thought that Peace had come / When peace was far away." She compares people to seafarers, who, thinking they see land symbolizing peace, are in the middle of the ocean: "That many fictious shores / Before the harbor lie." She was witness to the American Civil War, which claimed more victims than the United States suffered in all of its other conflicts combined, including the two World Wars. Should we quit there, with this bitter observation and tragic lesson, and cease meditating on peace, and take war for our topic, if it is the sole historical reality?

For, even thinkers of peace are not always reassuring. Hence Kant, for instance, who passionately denounces war and forms plans for perpetual peace, also sings the war song that runs through philosophy, evoking its potential "sublimity," and seeing it as the instrument of Providence. And the philosophical peace (that is, peace among philosophers) that he mentions at the end of his treatise on peace presupposes, on the part of the critical philosopher, a state of "permanent arms" (*immer bewaffneter*) against traditional metaphysics. The Kantian philosopher is, as we say nowadays, a "soldier of peace," yet a soldier all the same.

---

1. The preceding passage is David Horan's new English translation of Plato. See https://www.platonicfoundation.org/.

Should we not, then, take another approach, proffer a definition of peace that would not just be negative and privative, and think of it as something besides an absence of war? Philologists inform us that the name of "peace," with which Hebrews and Arabs as well greet one another, refers to something beyond non-aggression, the integrity and fulfillment of bodily and spiritual life, the safeguarding of the humanity in man. Those who ask for God to give them peace, or call for it from others, request more than the end of hostilities, but a concord and harmony that are exercised and deploy their positive actions. One of the Christian tradition's greatest attempts to define peace is summarized in chapter 13 of Book XIX of St. Augustine's *The City of God*. It is sometimes claimed that he gives ten different definitions, which would be too many! It is more accurate to say that he defines peace as "order's tranquility," regulated concord and harmony, a conception that unifies and brings together several terms, this unique definition applying to varying levels of reality, while still respecting their richness and diversity. An order cannot be defined apart from the nature of what it orders; peace for the dog is not the peace of man, peace in the home is not the peace of the state. Each level of being has (or could have) a "natural peace to its order" (XIX.12).

This definition of peace as *tranquillitas ordinis* will serve as a point of departure for a meditation on thinkers as diverse as St. Thomas Aquinas who, in his *Summa Theologica* (II, II, 29) or Luis de León, the great sixteenth-century Spanish poet and mystic, in his admirable work *The Names of Christ*, contemplate the title of Christ ("Prince of Peace") taken from Isaiah (9:5). Its apparent simplicity, which can almost be deceiving, at first sight hides its depth. There can be order without tranquility, when it is maintained by the force of permanent repression and omnipresent fear—violence against the violent may be entirely legitimate and necessary, but it does not engender peace in a positive sense, the double negative not producing an affirmative ("eye for an eye," "death to assassins," "no liberty for the enemies of freedom," etc.). There can be a tranquility without order too, such as what results from a public or private enemy—this is what some of the peoples conquered by ancient Roman imperialism reproached the famous *Pax Romana* for: they create a void, a desert, and they call it "peace."

Before drawing any conclusions, an important remark is in order. To those who seek peace and want to fight for it, to those who feel the constant urgency of the task, discussing its definition may appear to be a waste of time, and an unbearable delay for action. But vigilance over the meaning of words, safeguarding the correctness of language, is one of the first duties of peacemakers, and perhaps even chronologically the first. A famous saying asserts that the first casualty of war is the truth, and indeed lies, propaganda, and what we now call "disinformation" are some of the evils (and weapons) of war, as well as what leads to it. Analyzing the situation becomes a crime of defeatism. Before a war is ever declared, the increase in abuses of language is the indication announcing reason's eclipse. What did the Hitlerian word *Lebensraum*, "living space," mean? Nobody has described this better than Thucydides in the *History of the Peloponnesian War*, when discussing the civil war and its expansion: "We change the ordinary meaning of words for things in order to provide the justification we wish to give. An inconsiderate boldness passes for devoted courage to a cause, a circumspect prudence for hidden fear, wisdom for the mask of cowardice, wisdom in everything for complete laziness; rash impulsiveness is taken as genuine virtue, and careful deliberations as a beautiful excuse for secrets" (III.82.4). This passage struck Montaigne, who mentions it in his *Essays* (I.23).

Many testimonies reveal that one of the aspects of demoralization, even despair, following the end of the First World War involved the widespread feeling that the most noble words had been trivialized: "justice," "right," "civilization," "heroism," and even the name of "peace" (the famous "Never again," the war to end all wars) remained tainted, perhaps irreparably, by the appalling and pointless slaughter that they had been used to justify, and to disguise in a garb of nobility. It is therefore a duty to speak out, and always to speak justly.

To return to the positive Augustinian definition of peace, it is clear that in its rigor, it removes peace from historical time, and makes it an object of eschatological hope: only eternal life can be the place of total and complete peace. Peace in history is always local, partial, provisional, uncertain. In the world, we do not have (and cannot have) an experience of peace's measure in all its breadth, in all its joy and life. This is one aspect, even if only one, of the Pauline expression "the peace of God which surpasses all understanding" (Phil 4:7). This raises the most important question for current purposes: from what experiential place can we ourselves attempt to speak of peace but as a hope beyond time and the world? Can it be given to us truly in experience?

Wherever and however little it may be, in establishing and spreading it, the sole experience of peace resides in the act that consists in *making* it, in that of pacification. Those who have always experienced civil peace, owing to history's favor, have never experienced the fullness of peace, but merely the absence of war. In French, the expressions "make peace" (*faire la paix*) and "wage war" (*faire la guerre*) exhibit an unfortunate asymmetry, because while war is waged all the time, sometimes day and night, peacemaking seems to be a one-off action, something that consists of concluding a truce or a treaty, or preparing for them. But it is not the same in the realm of the spirit, where making peace must be an incessant daily task. If we cannot know complete peace in time by dwelling in it like a homeland, we can each and every day advance along "the path of peace" (Rom 3:17), accomplish "that which promotes peace" (Rom 14:17), and seek peace and pursue it (Ps 34:15). Peace exists in the world only through peacemakers,[2] and so long as they alone act. This is why the silencing, or even murder, of peacemakers is often the war before the war, an act preceding it, showing that the main enemy is not the enemy, but the peaceable, for those who want universal consent for a war must often equate the pacifist to a traitor for the sake of that cause.

Yet where does this path to peace begin? Does it originate in us, and is the first task of the peacemaker to find peace in himself? The question is as complex as it is decisive. For it is certainly obvious that a man who is internally torn and violent due to his passions and given over to irreconcilable contradictions cannot be the agent of pacification for others any more than self-hatred can be the source of love for others. However, on the other hand, reading the admirable pages of all the spiritual traditions on inner peace (which admittedly do not always speak of peace in the same sense), we cannot fail sometimes to experience discomfort, wondering at what exact price this peace must come, and whether that price might be one of indifference to the escalating groans of evil and sin. If interior peace consists in having the best of both worlds, and withdrawing "above the fray" into an inner fortress, doesn't it risk resembling those contemporary gated communities where walls, guards, dogs, and electronic systems protect the rich from outside violence, forming a plutocratic reserve like so-called nature parks? Is it not time again to cite Jeremiah: they say "Peace," when there is no peace?

2. The French term here, *les pacifiques*, could also be translated as "pacificists," but to ensure that the biblical resonance of the term in this context is not lost, I have chosen to render it as "peacemakers," given that this is the term that appears in many of the English translations of the Sermon on the Mount. Chrétien will turn to that biblical scene later in this chapter.

In what we call the Sermon on the Mount, Christ urgently exhorts us not to present an offering to God if we ourselves have not first of all been reconciled with our brother (Matt 5:23–24)—where it's crucial that this brother is he who holds a grudge against me, not the one I hold a grudge against. So, it's not a question of overcoming my own internal resentment, but of striving to assuage his, and accordingly taking an active step towards peace. The Letter to the Ephesians (4:26) examines this precept: "Let not the sun go down upon your wrath," which is perceptive, too, in that anger, left to its own devices, can only grow and inflame itself more and more, when in insomnia I rehash the offense of which I feel myself to be the victim, always discovering new aspects of it that make it worse, just as our tongue endlessly explores the aching tooth.

Incidentally, in the Christian tradition, as with the Jewish tradition, even when alone, never am I before God solely as an individual, separated from others, for I only pray as a member of a community ("*Our Father*"): there could be no peace with God that would be an isolated one, and that was unaccompanied by an effort to make peace with others. When questioning whether peace constitutes a special virtue, St. Thomas Aquinas responds negatively; it is not a virtue, but rather the fruit of it, an occurrence of charity. Peace is love's openness, its rays and extension. Just as at sunrise we see the dawn's light before we see the sun, so invisible charity lets itself be seen by the always inchoate clarity of peace. Luis de León, distinguishing three forms of it, peace with God, peace with self, and peace with others, strongly accentuates their interdependence, mutual engenderment, and reinforcement. Many spiritualities would certainly lay the emphasis on one of these forms of peace, rather than on others, as constituting the true gateway to the path to peace, yet peace would never be deep if it weren't tridimensional, and not striven for in these three spheres. The question of whether we should begin with the search for inner peace or with agreement with others is therefore poorly posed; nobody is unaware that conflicts with others disturb us intimately, just as internal strife disturbs relationships with others.

So, let's come back to the one firm cornerstone: the experience of peace resides in the act of making it, or accepting that it is occurring. The word "pacific" (*pacifique*), in the strict sense, which is not synonymous with "peaceful" (*paisible*), the who one makes peace (*eirènopoios* in Greek), is only found a single time in the New Testament (it is absent from the Septuagint, the Greek translation of the Hebrew Bible, even if one finds the corresponding verb) in the Beatitudes: "Blessed are the peacemakers, for they shall be called the sons of God" (Matt 5:9). The Epistle of James elaborates on the expression: "The fruit of righteousness is sown in peace by those who make peace" (3:18). Nevertheless, the term's rarity does not mean that what it designates is unimportant.

To put the emphasis on pacification clearly implies that war, in the broad sense, is always primordial in human history, whether that be struggle with God, war between one another, or strife within ourselves. Ever futural and improbable peace, when it comes to pass, is always precarious, and is not a condition (whether defined negatively or positively) from which we would begin and that we only would have to preserve, by struggling against what could make us deviate from it. Instead, it is the very point of hope and desire. And so, the path to peace is not one to be embarked and advanced on, even at the cost of great efforts, as if it were already there, lying before us in the world, but one that must be invented and forged, step by step. It is like being in the jungle, when with a machete we make our way through the thicket of luxuriant and dense vegetation preventing us from seeing anything beyond what lies a few feet ahead of us. This image already expresses the essential: namely, making peace is a battle and a struggle—the most difficult of all, because it is not a matter of exerting a strength that was already there, and that I would only have to learn to use, but of letting grow within me one naturally foreign to myself, that of peace. (Wanting tranquility, which often is our desire, is not at all identical to wanting true peace: I can lead a relatively peaceful life by not getting involved in anything, and by averting my eyes from the injustice committed around me.)

As Arthur Rimbaud puts it unforgettably in the final poem of *A Season in Hell*, "Spiritual warfare is as brutal as the wars of men." This is not to say that it uses the same means and weapons, this entails that it is another use of the same violence, but that it has its own violence, and no less so. Here, it is not an issue of debating its legitimacy, efficacy, or the necessity of what we call "non-violence" in political and social conflicts. In any case, it is meant as moral violence, as a shock to those who are confronted with it. What needs to be highlighted is the spiritual struggle for peace's extreme violence, which, being *sui generis* belongs to it alone. To be at peace, it is necessary to become capable of *incredible violence*; for to make peace, it is always necessary to make violence, individually and collectively. The angry man's cries and blows relieve and soothe his internal fuming, just as an insult or an inflicted humiliation diminishes his resentment over having lost face, by reestablishing him in a position of superiority. Violence's expansion and administration reveals fallen man's natural course; it is noteworthy that ancient philosophy wrote so much about wrath and techniques to overcome it. As we say, to take a slap in the face or a word of contempt without replying with even greater force is to achieve a victory over oneself, and so a violence against oneself—for peace.

Augustine, who meditated at such length and depth on peace, has an acute appreciation for all this. Till our last day on earth, we will have "internal enemies," he says in *Enchiridion* (XXIII.91)—in the form of our inveterate vices and sins. Having made the choice of unrighteousness, humanity has not desired peace with God, but "makes war upon itself," a beautiful passage says in *The City of God* (XXI.15). Yet "better is it to contend with vices than without conflict to be subdued by them. Better, I say, is war with the hope of peace everlasting than captivity without any thought of deliverance." Lack of resistance to evil is the triumph of evil—that does not mean it is a flaw to use its own weapons (a constant temptation and drama of history: even in just wars, one ends up using unjust means, and each side accuses the other of having introduce their use). It is true that the question is not posed in terms of inner struggle (at least not the struggle of one vice against another . . .).

Being the most difficult, the way of peace is also the most courageous, when it doesn't consist in allowing injustice to go unchecked ("Better Hitler than war"). But precisely here a question must be posed at great risk. Extolling inner struggle and victory over oneself has inspired many sublime pages that are as informative as they are invigorating. How beautiful it is to dream of ourselves as spiritual soldiers on the vanguard of peace, how moving it is to imagine ourselves (even in just an internal battle) as advance scouts behind enemy lines! There once was a pious and peaceable association, the "Legion of Mary," whose name is perplexing nonetheless. In this meditation on peace, we must therefore take another further step.

The experience of peace is to make it. To make it is to be reconciled. But the Bible affirms that reconciliation among men, as with oneself, is solely possible through a justice presupposing a divine action that reconciles them. It is St. Paul first and foremost who in the New Testament expounds and teaches the doctrine of reconciliation (*katallagè*). The verb "reconcile," in the relation between God and men, is always employed by him in the active voice for God and in the passive for men. "Be ye reconciled to God" (2 Cor 5:20): this is passive (the Jerusalem Bible translates it exactly like

Luther). It is not men who establish peace with God; it is God alone who grants peace to men and takes the initiative, so that men can make peace among themselves. It is Christ, "who is our peace," that in his passion, "his body slain enmity thereby" (Eph 2:14, 16), made possible unity among men who had been separated. We only make peace (forgiveness and reconciliation) by having already received it. Only those who receive God's forgiveness have a resource that can never fail them for forgiving others, provided that they continue to draw on it. The valor of human reconciliation is first founded on the creature's receptivity to the Creator.

We accordingly are never peace's engineers or demiurges, and the message of peace that we can bring is not the fruit of our own spirit; when we propose it, we are only the legates, the delegates, the ambassadors, according to the stirring Pauline expression: "Now then we are ambassadors for Christ, as though God did beseech you through us" (2 Cor 5:20). This is of the utmost importance, for these words mean that when we bring the word of peace, and the plan of making peace among ourselves, we are not asking others to bend and to submit to our own will (would that be reconciliation?), but we are announcing to them the possibility that we stand together (and therefore without conquering or being vanquished) in a peace that comes from above us, a peace that both the one proposing it and the one accepting it did nothing save receive. This certainly doesn't entail that man is merely passive, or that we are God's puppets. The same Letter to the Corinthians (6:1) speaks of synergy and cooperation with God. Receiving is also an action, without which no gift would be able to come to fruition or come to term. There is no way of fully explicating the Pauline thought of reconciliation here, and so a final question arises.

In the Bible, peace, which never can be considered apart from justice (another aspect of the Augustinian *tranquillitas ordinis*), always possesses an eschatological dimension. According to the words of Isaiah (11:6–7), it is not within historical time that the wolf shall lie down with sheep, the panther with the goat, or that the lion will eat grass with the ox (on an allegorical interpretation, at least, some church fathers have viewed these animals as representations of human temperaments). Doomed to perpetual wars that would sometimes be terrible, sometimes latent, sometimes "cold" and sometimes burning, does this mean that humanity would merely have to resign itself to the painful expectation of a peace only to come after death? Certainly not, for that would be to rest hope on despair, and so on quicksand.

For Christian faith, such hope turns on death and resurrection. As St. Paul says of Christians, we appear "as dying, and behold, we live" (2 Cor 6:9). Baptism raises us in Christ, yet it does not deliver us from having to die. Faith is already a participation in eternal life (St. Thomas Aquinas describes it well as a "foretaste"), but it doesn't remove us out of time. Similarly, the fullness of peace in justice will only happen in eternal life, yet it begins here and now, with reconciliation's time. With each deed done here and now with an eye to this end, whether it be a historically significant matter between two peoples, or something small between two individuals, a living eternity begins. We hear the discreet and new pulse of eternal life beating in each gesture where men grant each other forgiveness, and imagine a future that hatred could never have anticipated. The reverse is well known to men of war, whose abominable acts are not necessarily the result of blind, unthinking violence, but of a diabolical deliberation: they commit the irreparable so that there can be no turning back, and so that not only war rages on, but future peace becomes unthinkable (this is the hope of the despairing). Every time peace is made and reconciliation takes place, the dawn of eternity rises above history's shadows, and the reign of the Prince of Peace acquires a bridgehead in us. This involves peace in a positive sense, the form of which is not just an interruption of hostilities owing to the exhaustion or ruin of the combatants, but at least a partial victory over hatred, and a promise of cooperation. For us, peace's high noon begins with candles lit in the night (a candle can be seen from father away and shines brighter than we think), yet it is already the light as such. Let us give due credit to Shakespeare for this image:

> *How far that little candle throws his beams!*
> *So shines a good deed in a naughty world.*

("Naughty" derives from "naught," nothingness: in viewing evil as a form of nonbeing, Portia is thus an Augustinian without knowing it.)[3]

---

3. Portia is the rich, beautiful, and intelligent female protagonist of *The Merchant of Venice.*

Meditation 8

Gentleness

IN ORDER TO EVOKE gentleness,[1] should we merely touch lightly on its being, prepare ourselves to murmur caressing words, and so first purify our voice of all sharpness, obduracy, all excessive forcefulness, or, in a word, mitigate it, since *mitigare* in Latin, coming from *mitis*, does indeed mean to soften? Or proceed by circuitous insinuations and short tangents, as approaching it head-on seems decidedly too brutal? To adopt an unctuous and soothing patina-like expression, however, would certainly be to spoil the task. Too much gentleness no longer is sweet, but only nauseating. Verlaine, the poet of sweetness he is, says it well in one of the "Watercolors" of his *Songs without Words*: "The sky was too blue, too tender, / The sea too green and the air too mild (*doux*)."[2] And you, dear reader, certainly don't want a sappy postcard, but a gently chiseled engraving.

Verlaine's is the sad, muted sweetness of the lonely heart, not the deep, joyful kind we're here to ponder. The *Poems under Saturn* evoke the former often, as in "Lassitude": "With sweetness, with sweetness, with sweetness!" he asks the "lover," wanting to possess her, leaving him in "feverish rapture" and "the quiet forgetfulness of a sister," as he weeps all night. And in "Sunsets": "The melancholy / Refrain of sweet songs, / My

1. The meditation's title "Gentleness" (*Douceur*) can in French also mean "sweetness," "softness," and "mildness," depending on context. This polysemy is captured, to some extent, by the English "meekness," a word Chrétien will mention later in this meditation.

2. Debussy, the French composer and pianist, set some of Paul Verlaine's poems, such as "Clair de lune," to music. Here, Chrétien quotes verses from the latter's poem, "Spleen," which was subsequently set to piano in the six-piece song cycle, "Forgotten Songs" (*Ariettes oubliées*), as "No. 6: Aquellere II: Spleen." The connection between music and Verlaine's poetry is mentioned in passing elsewhere. See *Hand to Hand*, 54.

heart forgetting." In one of the most famous and admirable of the *Ariettes oubliées* (again in *Songs without Words*), the poet addresses himself to the source of "languor": "Oh the sweet sound of rain / On the pavement and on the roofs! / For a languishing heart, / Oh the song of the rain!"[3] It is with this line of Verlaine's that Paul-Jean Toulet will evoke the danger of sweetness in the first of his *Chansons*: "In Arles, where the Alescans are, / When the shade is red underneath the roses, / And the air clear, / Beware the sweetness of things."[4] Sweetness can wound the heart, and entirely undo such a caliber of man through trials. And yet, Verlaine himself knew there existed an altogether different sweetness besides the one which overwhelms him and prompts his song, for, in *Amour*, he praises Calderón as "That terrific and divinely sweet poet."

How is it possible to be fierce and gentle simultaneously? It must be, however, for in order to be a virtue, gentleness must not merely soften us, dull us, enfeeble us, for then it would not at all constitute a virtue. As with nearly every good philosophical question, it has been formulated by Plato. The second book of his *Republic* (375 BC) shows the necessity of the guardians for the just city, whose conditions of possibility, as mentioned, is to unite "natural spiritedness and natural gentleness." If they are just gentle, the guardians will protect nothing; if they are merely harsh, there will be violence, even savagery, in short order. Uniting the two appears to be an impossibility. Nonetheless, to find a solution, we need look no further than to the tip of our nose, if that nose happens to be in front of a snout, for the good housedog is gentle with visitors and fierce with intruders. (For Plato, the philosopher in his hunt for Being must have a rambunctiousness worthy of a dog, and the German word *suchen* comes from the vocabulary of the chase.) And if you don't care for dogs, don't worry! For there is Theaetetus, whose portrait we are provided at the beginning of Plato's eponymous dialogue.

This young man certainly is not handsome (even if he himself is not so ugly as Socrates), however, he learns well that "gentleness, on the other hand, is exceptional; and to all this he joins an incomparable valor (that is,

3. This is not the only work of Chrétien's in which Verlaine's poem, "Il pleure dans mon cœur," receives attention. See, for example, *Hand to Hand*, 154.

4. Paul-Jean Toulet (1867–1920), French poet and novelist most famous for the work of poems *Les contrerimes*. The work in which Toulet's poem "En Arles" appears, is a reference to the genre of *Chansons de geste*, Old French for "a song of heroic deeds." *Alescans*, the inspiration for Toulet's poem, is a piece of twelfth-century epic poetry that recounts a fictional battle in which the Christian army was defeated by the Saracen army.

in Greek, virility and courage); in short, a combination of qualities that I wouldn't have thought possible, and not seen elsewhere" (*Theaetetus* 144A). And, a little further on, of the form of movement that warrants study and investigation, namely, continuous moment, it is said with no false misstep to be "a great gentleness" resembling "the silent stream of oil" (144B). Here is not the place to examine whether Theaetetus will exhibit all the promises he is said to bear, but his figure illustrates the question well.

This latter figure is not only sketched in the profane sphere, but also in the highest places of revelation as well. In fact, the same Greek word for gentleness (*praotès*) that Plato uses is present in the Holy Bible to describe Moses, and Jesus applies it to himself. The Septuagint, the official version of the first Christian church, indeed says that "the man Moses was the meekest of all" (Num 12:3). Too often translations say "humble" rather than "gentle," but, as we have seen, the two terms are neighbors in the Bible, and in English it reads as "very meek," which combines the two. Reading many biblical episodes, such as Moses's vision of Archangel Michael, will redirect our eyes to Verlaine's expression, "terrible and divinely gentle." As for Jesus, he says in Matthew, "learn of me, for I am meek and lowly of heart" (11:29), a word that will serve as the inspiration for all Christian meditations on meekness.

In the chapter "Agneau" of *Names of Christ* (a chapter added to the posthumous edition), Luis de León cites the first word in order to illustrate that "Lamb" means "gentleness" (*mansedumbre*, the root of our French *mansuétude* ["gentleness"]). Yet he comes quickly to the question: how can the Lamb at the same time be the Lion, the Lion of Judea referenced in Revelation 5:5? And as Luis de León shows, there is no contradiction despite initial appearances. It is because he's the meek lamb to his own that he is the lion against the powers of evil and hell: he is *fiero*, ferocious, cruel, as many of the mystics put it, because he is *manso*, gentle towards those whom he protects and defends. In his lengthy and beautiful (he does not use the word) abyssal word: "the wrath of the Lamb" (*orgè tou arniou*, Rev 6:17). (It is in order to flee from this wrath that the world's mighty men will beg the mountains to topple over them.) The insurrection of light against darkness is the most irresistible of all, the wrath of the Lamb the most spirited, for it originates from the very power of affirmation itself.

Let's descend from these dizzying heights to which we were so speedily carried up and away like smoke, and let us return more modestly to this force that gentleness must harness, in every sense of the term, if it is to be truly itself. Proust noted well in the psychological terms that are his: "The rule [. . .] is that the hard are the weak whom nobody wanted, and the strong, caring little whether anybody wanted them or not, have alone this gentleness that the vulgar mistake for weakness" (*Sodom and Gomorrah*, II.3). Flaubert's *Sentimental Education* (I.6) already described Frédéric Moreau as "weary, enervated, overcome at last by the terrible force of comfort (*douceur*)" (at issue is his mother). Yet the philosophical tradition as much as the theological has ruminated on this for a long time. Aristotle in the *Nicomachean Ethics* (IV.11) emphasized that, while gentleness is to be praised, the meek man also knows how to be a man of anger, a righteous and sober anger, in which he is neither overwhelmed nor carried away. And Christian authors have equated humility with magnanimity, to the noble soul, powerful and generous, foreign to dishonorable timidity by which we profane the image of God in us. A soft sweetness lacking firmness would soon dissipate, like a psychological vapor, like a humor giving way to sourness. This is a great theme of St. Francis de Sales, for example, a thoroughly gentle man, who, invites one of his correspondents to behave "so that your courage is humble and your humility courageous" (*Letter* 1524), in the broad and vivid sense courage has in the classical vernacular. We always come across Plato's demand in other places.

That gentleness must be strong does not yet tell us what it is. The traditional philosophical framework for the virtuous traits undoubtably accords the latter too narrow a perspective (which still is detectable in St. Thomas Aquinas's *Summa Theologica* [IIa IIae, q157] treatment of it, along with clemency): gentleness appears above all to be a corrective and a restraint, mastery and control over anger, the fact that it not does not let itself be carried away. Yes, yet does this suffice to define it fully? Ancient and medieval moral theory define the virtues by the nature of the actions they enact, by the inclinations within us that they regulate, and by the faculties they enable us to exercise. However, if we consider the extraordinary semantic expansion of the word "gentleness" (*douceur*) in French (you only have to open a dictionary to read the list of its antonyms), does it go without saying that it pertains only to a specific region of our life and action? Is it one single act that, whatever the object, can't be said to have been performed with or without it? Does gentleness involve the content of our actions or their mode? Does it pertain to *what* is done, or *how* is it done?

Gentleness lies in virtue of the *how* and of the *manner*, but to be sure, as Kierkegaard insisted on this term in his existential thought, the *how* determines the *what* in turn, and cannot be separated from it, for it is what displays itself as it gives itself to be seen. Gentleness presupposes self-mastery (St. Paul mentions it as a fruit of the Holy Spirit in Galatians 5:23 alongside self-control), and certainly not just over anger. This is why undeniably it is not without strength: the gentle man is he who emerges victorious from battle with himself. It does not suffice, however, for this victory over evil to be soft: do not get angry, do not contest everything, do not interrupt, do not show sweetness but merely courtesy. We can agree curtly and disapprove sweetly, we can speak with love brusquely and frankly, we can speak with a sweetness that is not shared. Yet these acts of gentleness can take many forms, by merely refraining from wounding, or opening themselves up to something higher.

It is therefore necessary to bring to light its positive dimension. Gentleness *lets be* what (or whom) it finds itself before, in order to take time for it. It does not take this time from others, but from and of itself, and thereby gives it to others. Would it be a gentle one were the word not first preceded by the patience of listening? And would it be meek were it not first attentive? A sweet look, for example, does not involve "sweet eyes" (sentimental or sexual seduction in which one takes the initiative), but in making our presence a place of welcoming and hospitality—letting go, without hate or prevention, so that somebody may show up (or something, for there is also a gentleness towards things and places). Wanting to speak gently is to do so slowly, with attention and precaution. It is the strength of gentleness to divine the fragility of people, things, and questions tenderly. For there is a gentleness of thought also that does not brutalize phenomena, neither the words by which we name them, nor does it want to be a conqueror, removing by force a curtain or partition—what Plato designated with his customary rigor when likening the intellectual approach of Theaetetus to the slow silent streaming of oil. In matters of thought, advancing brutally seriously risks rendering us merely masters over a field of ruins: having first dissected, dismembered, and destroyed what we wished to think, we are certainly free to say and do what we want, and to be intoxicated with the sound of our own voice and its thunderous proclamations.

Precisely because it comes to disarm, unguarded gentleness obtains everything it does as it demands nothing, nothing definite, nothing graspable, except that we give ourselves over to it, even to the point of self-abandonment. All this, which is inexhaustible, clearly makes it fraternal with humility, for we cannot imagine a humility without gentleness or a gentleness without humility. Yet the two are not to be confused with each other, for their original site is not identical: humility in the strict sense is first and essentially before God, just as pride is a revolt against God that makes the self its own idol, while gentleness is first and essentially concerned with the other and finite things. There is, to be sure, a gentleness of God, but does it make sense to speak of my own gentleness or harshness towards God? These observations immediately raise a question: is there a gentleness towards oneself, or can it only concern my relations to others? In his *Introduction to the Devout Life*, St. Francis de Sales follows his chapter, "On Gentleness towards Neighbor and Remedies against Anger," with another titled "On Gentleness towards Ourselves" (III.9).

"One good practice to make of gentleness," he says, "is with respect to ourselves, never getting angry with ourselves or our imperfections." This certainly is not an avoidance of or exemption from repentance, but rather a healthy criticism of the latter's perversion, whereby it would turn (as we say that milk turns) "bitterly unpleasant and chagrined, vexatious and angry" (this classical use of "anger" as an adjective has only been preserved in colloquial language, particularly in the South). "There are many," Francis explains, "who, having gotten angry, fall into the error of being angry because they were angry, and enter into grief over being chagrined and are irritated over being vexed; for in this manner, they harden their heart and drown in wrath." He underscores the privileged connection to anger, but the structure, as we all know from our experience, is actually more general: I am disappointed with having been disappointed, weakened over having been weak, obsessed with having had an obsession, full of fear for having been afraid, and so on. This is not a struggle against evil, but at bottom, a reinforcing and intensification of it, inviting new stumbles, by putting the focus, as St. Francis shows so well, on the humiliations done to our self-regard, and not the work of repentance. (With uneven success, I recommend to students whose anxiety undermines their ability to take exams, not to ruminate on one bad test if they don't want to make it a law and an inevitability.)

For, as he adds, the discontentment we experience over some fault that bothers us, leaves us in a state of overindulgence (even blindness) to those that don't matter as much to us, and that don't seem as bad in our own eyes. "Thus, when our heart has committed some mistake, if we reprove it with gentle and calm admonitions, having compassion rather than anger for it, encouraging it to amend," this almost fatherly gentleness will bear more fruit than will a fit of anger against oneself. Wise, just, and gentle counsel! Far from leading to self-indulgence and complacency, such gentleness towards oneself paves the only way for escaping egocentric complacency, which has both negative and positive forms. Loving others as oneself implies that we can treat, in Paul Ricœur's beautiful phrase, "oneself as another," and hence with gentleness. This gentleness is not a resolution we make to ourselves, but a living way lying on a tangent outside the futile circularity, like a frantic hamster in its cage, of our thoughts and lives.

The scarcity of words is sometimes impoverishing, sometimes enriching, and sometimes the unexpected wealth of poverty itself. This is how French uses one and the same word to describe the biblical virtue of gentleness, which in English is expressed as "meekness" (as we have seen for Moses, but also it is the word for the gentleness of Christ), the gentleness of a fabric we touch ("soft"), that of a weather's climate or food dish ("mild"), that of an approach or manners ("gentle"), that of a perfume, a melody, or honey ("sweet"), and the list goes on. We certainly also have *suave* (from the same root as the English sweet and the German *süss*): St. Bernard of Clairvaux, as it happens, speaks of *dulcedo suavitalis*, sweet suavity, which, in removing one of the terms, translators take to be a pleonasm, although it is a specification: a sweetness that is of the order of suavity, and thus tasted and felt. Yet we would not speak of the virtue of being suave! As a result, thanks to this transit ticket that is the word "gentleness," like in French as in Latin, we move easily and gently, passing from one realm to another, retaining in one the memory of the other.

This is how "sweetness" becomes a divine name, which, when applied to the Lord of worlds, is stupefying and astounding. In Book I of his *Confessions*, St. Augustine uses the term evocatively several times when addressing himself to God (there are many other examples from his later work and elsewhere in his oeuvre): "My God, my life, my holy sweetness" (I.4.4), "My sweetness, my God" (I.6.9), and in the final lines of the same book: "Thank you my sweetness, my strength, and my confidence, my God, thank you for all your gifts" (I.19.31). God's name is immediately preceded and followed by that of "sweetness." Before considering its meaning, we must pay attention to the circumstances of its usage. This is not the name of God in isolation, but of God for us, with us, and within us. It refers to what happens in God's presence when God meets us. God's sweetness can only be uttered in confession, prayer, praise, *dulcedo mea*. The possessive adjective announces that such sweetness takes possession of us, and that it will not become our property. It appears only in the space between God and us, in gift and gratitude. We could not profess that "God is sweet" in the same way we do "God is love," even if one is only the consequence and sign of the other. This name names God as the source of what I experience, feel, and do, as we can see in the parallel of "trust" (*confiance*). It's no vapid or sentimental term, for it can be used in discussions where the focus is God's greatness, power, and majesty as Creator.

Yet where, and how, does this sweetness reveal itself? By what means can we come to taste it? The Word of God itself tells us that this gentleness is given first and forever in God's Word: "How sweet are thy words unto my taste, Yea, sweeter than honey to my mouth," says the vast oratorio of the Law (Ps 119:103). Without using the word, the Letter to the Hebrews speaks of those who "have tasted the good word of God and the powers of the world to come" (6:5). God's sweetness is *necessarily* first and foremost a matter of his word (often compared by the church fathers, especially Origen, to the miraculous "manna" of the Hebrews in the wilderness, which takes on all sorts of flavors on the tongue, and is what I need, here and now, to remake myself), for without it (which is a "lamp to my feet," says the psalm a little later) I would be unable to know that this taste I experience is one of the sweetness *of God*. This taste has nothing unappealing about it, like with dishes that are initially tasty and then become nauseating on a second helping. It may be that we do not sense it, and what will be sweet may previously have been tasteless, even bitter, yet once this sweetness is experienced it is unforgettable (even if we are embittered over not tasting it again). Its unforgettable character resides in the fact that this word is the future's word alone, of the future absolutely speaking, namely that of eternal life. And this future that it promises is already surfacing in those droplets of light—and night also, according to the words of the Song of Songs (5:2)—that are the Bible's words. But taste is an act of ours for which we ourselves must prepare, and that also prepares us.

That is why God is not sweetness, but as the case may be, as St. Augustine says, "my sweetness," or ours. It takes a palate and a throat for sweetness to reveal itself. The "meekness of wisdom" spoken of in the dazzling Epistle of James ([3:14], amid an analysis of sweet and bitter) cannot be attained without patience and training. The Word's sweetness and that of what it speaks, by definition, cannot be immediate. Augustine makes much of the words of Psalm 31:20 invoking the superabundant majesty of divine kindness that God "hides those who fear him" (*Sur le psaume* XXX.

IV.6). That God hides is preparation for any genuine wisdom, because it means he holds in reserve the divine sweetness while the mouth of our hearts is purified and educated by fear.

Will, however, it be the case that we are up to such a task, or is our palate spoiled and damaged so irremediably that perhaps we will never come to receive and taste this food? Augustine answers this question with another word of the Psalmist (Ps 21:3), by affirming that God warns and instructs "with the blessings of goodness (*douceur*)." He states vehemently that "the blessing of sweetness is God's grace, by which is caused in us that what pleases and arouses our desire—that is, what we love—is what He prescribes" (*Against Two Letters of the Pelagians*, II.9.21). When I joyfully do something righteous because it is righteous, or even when I have joy in intending to do it, such is "the blessing of sweetness" that God alone can bestow. Only sweetness readies our bitter palate by infusing it with the desire to taste righteousness. In the final page of *A Season in Hell*, Arthur Rimbaud says, "the sight of justice is the delight of God alone." Yet the taste of righteousness is a delight God shares. It is grace's sweetness. And being the very act that frees us, it is absurd to oppose that grace to freedom. Far from diminishing or revoking the latter, grace restores it to us.

Such sweetness certainly is not a sugary confection, not some spiritual candy (which more than anything rots the spirit's teeth). For if righteousness is for us insipid or bitter, how then would we possess the strength and courage to battle for it till the end? We all know the bitterness and acridness when our friends or we ourselves are the victims of injustice (or at least when we think so), just as we know justice's sweetness when it is done or offered to us. What, however, happens when the sweetness of righteousness does not widen or expand, when our taste stops with nothing more than seeing justice done for us, or seeing it done to those with whom we ourselves sympathize? The fiery pepper of vengeance and resentment always inflames that raw passion German calls *Rechthaberei*, the desire always to be right to the point of thwarting justice, as captured by the Latin maxim *Summum jus, summa injuria* (extreme justice is extreme injustice). Kleist's novella *Michael Kohlhaas* (1810)[5] exemplarily dramatizes the desire through the story of a man who, finding himself the victim of a minor breach of his rights, ends up embroiled in a bloody battle to obtain justice.

---

5. Bernd Heinrich Wilhelm von Kleist (1777–1811), German poet, dramatist, and novelist.

It is gentleness's strength as a virtue not to know these limits and hindrances, to acquire a taste for justice always and everywhere. And if the meek shall inherit the earth (Matt 5:5), that is because the gentle are at home wherever justice is done (just as we say of fine weather being as sweet as home), something that can be attained only in the fight for hope. This taste is not a savor that we would keep for ourselves, for the oil of sweetness comes to expand itself surely and silently, offering and sharing itself. Filling this inexhaustible jar in a few pages is certainly out of the question.

So, we'll conclude with the discreet thought that gentleness is *welcoming*. It is so, because it permits coming and going, removes partitions, porticoes, obstacles, and fortifications, granting free access to our presence and our gaze, as well as to our ear: the meek man keeps his attention's table uncluttered. Gentleness lets itself be entered only because it itself is piercing: its slowness and discreetness insinuate themselves almost everywhere. It belongs to gentleness to be considerate, and not to need to be petitioned, but to anticipate what is demanded lovingly. Yet this hospitality for the other is itself possible only because it has received and welcomed what permits it to be so, the Holy Spirit. The Latin hymn "Come, Holy Spirit" includes the word "sweet" twice: "The soul's sweet guest, the pilgrim's sweet relief" (*Dulcis hospes animae, Dulcis refrigerium*). With the same act of his presence, he alone gives both gentleness and strength at once. Are any of the subsequent prayers fitting for the request of gentleness?

We could with good reason suggest such is the case with *Flecte quod est rigidum*, "Bend what is inflexible" (of what is within us).[6] Gentleness, indeed, belongs essentially to the flexibility enabling its mobility. An inflexible man is not necessarily unjust, yet we immediately sense the incompatibility between firmness and gentleness, as we know that toughness will never make us love or taste the savor of justice. Relaxing also means softening up. The strength of gentleness does not consist in being unshakeable, but rather in moving with ease and versatility. It goes round what cannot be attacked head-on, it takes by surprise, it does not use the same weapons as its adversary, but renders them inoperable. So, let's start by suppling up. For, as Angelus Silesius says in *The Cherubinic Wanderer* (III.142), "in gentleness God dwells."

---

6. This verse is from the prayer "Veni Sancte Spiritus." Sometimes referred to as the "Golden Sequence," the prayer is used in the Roman Liturgy for the Masses of Pentecost.

Meditation 9

Abandonment

HEGEL SAW ONE OF the superiorities of German over other modern languages in the fact that some of its words have not only varying, but strongly opposed, meanings. It is a "joy for thought," he said, to come across such words, which manifest in "naïve fashion" the union of opposites in everyone's vocabulary. This union, which is absurd only to an understanding as narrow as it is rigid, tense about alternatives, is what leads to what he calls "speculation," grand reason's highest exercise (1831 preface to *The Science of Logic*). He himself, with the word *Aufhebung*, signifying both the act of conserving and of surpassing, made this joy one of his thought's guiding threads.

The word "abandonment" (*abandon*),[1] peculiar to the Romance languages even though it is not of Latin derivation, offers us this joyful thought profusely, although it can quickly become shrouded with anxiety, as the unity of its opposing meanings is not at all guaranteed. We have in French *abandon*, Spanish and Portuguese *abandono*, Italian *abbandóno*, and English has borrowed from us. The various acceptations being neither ancient Greek, Latin, or German, it cannot be translated by a single term. Its primary sense is that of a voluntary transfer, a handing over, of something to someone, typically through a legal act. What I relinquish is no longer mine,

---

1. As Chrétien's ensuing examination of the word will highlight, *abandon* can also mean "desertion," "forsaken," "letting go," "relinquishment," or "surrender" (an especially tempting translation for this chapter's title, given the surrounding chapters' at once martial and spiritual focus [peace, gentleness, and wound]), among other things. Although English expressions like "He pursued his goal with reckless abandon" do use the word as a noun, typically it is used as a verb. Because the French *abandon* is a noun, the chapter title has been translated into English as "abandonment."

and it no longer is up to me to care for it. I leave it, abandon it, and I no longer care about it. Yet we do not only abandon things or places, for we can also abandon someone and even ourselves.

What's more, abandonment can have an active as well as a passive sense, just as it can also denote an action or a condition: it can refer just as much to the act by which I abandon something, as it can to the situation in which I find myself when I have been abandoned, or in which something no longer matters to anyone. Furthermore, I can quit caring for something because I have given it up to someone else, or because I no longer want anything to do with it, and let it fall into ruins. Abandoning myself can mean confiding in someone and handing myself over to their care, or not caring about myself at all, by no longer looking out for myself. Something forgotten lies deserted. (Forgetting oneself has opposing meanings: I can forget myself owing to generosity and sacrifice, but also in insolence and presumption, to say nothing of weakness!). And additionally, in old French, self-forgetting (*soi abandoner*) can mean "to throw oneself headlong into a battle, without reserve and with all one's strength," as with the adverb "recklessly" (*abandoneement*).

Accordingly, this word refers us to what is noblest as well as to what is most lowly, to elevations above oneself as well as to the collapse and loss of self, to what is most joyous as well as to what is most tragic. Love abandons itself, yet so does melancholy, understood in the psychiatric sense. Holiness is a form of abandonment, yet so too is damnation. No speculation would be able to unite these two senses, or so at least we might assume.

Let's begin with one of its meanings that is most salient in daily life. Negligence is a carelessness whereby I don't care (or care little) about something and do not watch over or guard it. It can be the height of elegance or charm (what could be more seductive than what used to be called a feminine "nightgown" [*négligé*]), as well as vulgarity or sleaziness.

Elegance can be found solely in freedom and ease, when one is not dressed to the nines, and the most attractive outfits are not the most tailored nor the most openly styled, as in the case of the "deconstructed" dresses of the great couturiers. The Italian Renaissance extolled *sprezzatúra*, the art of hidden gracefulness, of appearing natural and spontaneous, which demands great care in appearing effortless.

Self-forgetful gestures and speech have this same grace, which in addition is always a sister of trust. We don't monitor ourselves with our friends as we would with others. There is a natural freedom through which we are spared from having to listen to our own words and watch what we do, just as we are also delivered from worrying about any judgment that might be passed on us. A friendship that did not involve talking freely would not be one. And the carefreeness of such surrender (*abandon*) is also one by means of which we are delivered from the restless, fastidious observance of rules, and thereby attain a higher freedom, as often evinced in the ultimate works of old painters or writers, who no longer have to prove themselves— which doesn't mean that they've lost their exactingness, but that they place it beyond convention, and free it, according to Rimbaud's phrase, "from common approval." In Chateaubriand's *La Vie de Rancé*, in Faulkner's *The Reivers*, or in the case of the aging Claudel (who comments on the Bible every morning, mixing memories of his sister and travel stories in a rickety coach), there is an extraordinary, admirable abandonment.

Carefreeness, after all, in the strict sense of lack of concern, is not at all wholly identical to carelessness. No longer paying attention to ourselves can be the condition of supreme attention by which something is done and seen. Surrender before a friend is confidence in him, and thus rests on looking to him. In spoken language, "letting-go" has the same ambivalence: the entire issue is knowing where we go when we let ourselves go, and how we get there. And in depression or melancholy's forlornness, there is the complete opposite of forgetfulness, the haunting of our own guilt, deficiency, or worthlessness. We let ourselves slide, yet we do not let go. To the letting-go that is trust's brother belongs simplicity's grace, whether that be in the friend or in the call of the task to be done, one affirming with an urgent silence its movement towards existence, a simplicity whose actions do not curl over themselves, but unfurl straight onward without having to heed where they are taking their next step, with an unreflective assurance and as if lovingly divinatory.

Yet if this first sense of abandonment involves self-forgetfulness and has the character of offering a figuration of self-nakedness, it nevertheless needn't entail the renunciation of self or one's ego. The latter is evoked by Pierre Corneille,[2] in his very beautiful poetic rendering of *The Imitation of Jesus-Christ* (which is a shame not to read), when he attributes to God this speech: "Leave, resign yourself, leave yourself behind" (III.27); the "resignation" does not here at all mean the disenchanted acceptance that our desire is not master over reality (which some psychiatrists view as the essence of alcoholism), but rather in the strong juridical and spiritual

2. Pierre Corneille (1606–84), French tragedian and dramatist.

sense, prevalent at the time, of surrender and desertion. To be resigned is to abandon oneself to God,[3] to leave one's "self" without reserve, and, at the very least, to have the intention of not returning.

Abandonment admits of highly opposed meanings in the religious domain as well. The abandonment of God can just as well refer to the act by which I abandon God as the one by which God abandons me. The abandonment of God is what we have since Nietzsche improperly called the "death of God" (a hijacking of the Christian vision of the passion). That the Bible and theology maintain adamantly, to the point of making it an adage, that God abandons only those who abandon him, and that he never takes the initiative, is essential, yet this does not constitute much of an immediate consolation, nor an instantaneously effective balm for whoever feels himself to be abandoned, because I myself must undertake the act of crying out to him from the depths of despair in which I find myself chained and bound. And, in so doing, it is imperative that I agree to abandoning myself to his promise, even though the abyss is precisely the non-place where it seems that the clarity of the promise, of any promise, whether from God, from others or myself, can no longer shine, and can no longer be expected or conceived.

Yet these various meanings are not simply juxtaposed. They communicate in different fashions. For what is the heart-wrenching core of the suffering of being abandoned? When the other leaves me, I am handed over to myself, I no longer have recourse to the other nor to another strength other than my own, and it is then that I discover who I am when I am only alone with myself. To be forsaken by others is to be abandoned to oneself. Abandonment's distress is a suffering in which I suffer myself. (But to abandon the other or God comes back to choosing to be abandoned to oneself, the prideful jubilation of being delivered from all promises and relying only on oneself, which, through the fire of its artifice, appears for a time like the opening to a festival of possibilities, only sooner or later to reveal itself to be at bottom emptiness.) It is with the word "abandonment" that Pascal

3. The word *abandon* retains echoes in French of the words *don* ("gift") and *donné* ("given"). Chrétien comments on this associative interplay among words elsewhere: "Words call out to one another and answer one another through intricate associative echoes, ceaselessly at play," *Call and Response*, 17. In French phenomenological philosophy there is the term *l'adonne*, coined by Jean-Luc Marion, to name someone who has abandoned himself to God—the so-called "gifted" or the "devoted." Chrétien is alluding to this spiritual valence of the term *abandon* here when highlighting how giving oneself up to God, letting-go or surrendering, involves a radical act of self-renunciation, self-desertion, or self-abnegation.

characterized "the blindness and wretchedness of man" bereft of God, "man without light left to himself, and, as it were, lost in this corner of the universe without knowing who has placed him there, what he has come to do, what will become of him at death" (*Pensées*, 693). Hell is me, me left to myself, to my own emptiness and my own dark disarray.

Another site of communication among abandonment's many senses is the ordeal of dryness, of absence and of darkness, which innumerable mystics have described as the highest purification, "passive" purification, according to the expression of St. John of the Cross, which is to say, where it is no longer I through my own efforts that transforms myself, but God himself who works in me. The very one who has embarked on the path of surrender to God can feel neglected and forsaken in the sharpest and most heartrending way. Father Grou, in the eighteenth century, said of the soul: "God leads it in this way from precipice to precipice, until finally it is brought to the edge of a great abyss, and is encouraged to throw itself over with a generous abandon" ("De l'abandon," *Manuel des âmes intérieures*). It is a matter of accepting this feeling of God's silence and absence within me, and of offering this blind consent as the ultimate offering I can make of myself, without being able to rely on the foresight of the One who welcomes it.

For the Christian mystics, the supreme expression of all these terrible descriptions is surely Christ's "dereliction" on the cross. The word comes to French from the Latin *derelinquere*, abandonment in the sense of neglect or desertion (*Verlassen* in German). It refers to one of the words of Christ on the cross, quoted in Hebrew before being translated, according to the Gospels of Matthew (27:46) and Mark (15:34): "My God, my God, why hast thou forsaken me?" This scene, the entirety of whose aspects is not possible to study here, uniquely brings together the two meanings of the word "abandonment." These words quote the opening ones of Psalm 22. The ample prayer of the latter, a torn and wrested call, begins with distress and ends with hope, starts with abandonment and ends in trust. The God who at the beginning is distant becomes the intimate God by the end. Many of its expressions prophesy of the passion (the thirst, the offenses, the parting of garments). And Jesus's *incipit* utterance arouses the very thing that the psalm says: sneering and mockery in the face of the one who invokes a God who does not come to help. The psalm therefore truly passes from one sense of abandonment to the other, thereby accomplishing the union of opposites. At the limit of anguish and of absence, God can come to us with an unparalleled closeness at the very moment in which we had felt we no longer had hope. There is a sort of death of the soul preceding the body's own, from which God resurrects us as well.

What would remain of the meaning or worth of trusting self-abnegation, if it were merely exercised at serene moments, and not especially so in times of night's darkness? In the simplest form of trust in human relations, it is precisely when the other seems to neglect or betray us, or ceases to be our friend, that confidence must transcend what appearance otherwise suggests. Yet in the interpretation of this word of Christ, we must keep hold of both ends of abandonment's chain. Taking into account the uttered words alone, without doubt, of course, indicates only the terror and neglect felt in the lowest depths of Christ's human soul: in the seventeenth century, in particular, there were among both Protestants and Catholics alike commentaries of unprecedented violence and virtual complacency toward the predilection for unsupportable statements evoking the wrath of the Father falling like lightning on the sins of humanity that Jesus bears in our place. Remembering the entire psalm and the response to its initial call, others instead tend to minimize and almost dissolve the primacy of the opening words (this is the current, though certainly not unanimous, tendency today). Abandonment *to* God alone unites the two meanings of act and movement: the coming of God's breath in the painful shortness of that felt absence, the lightning flash of its proximity passing through the veil of faraway clouds.

Before deepening this dimension, let us meditate on the great philosopher Schelling, who, it is true, inspired by mysticism down to the detail of his expression, thought, and impassioned language, held that true initiation into philosophy could occur exclusively by way of radical dereliction, like a naked swimmer who, with nothing, leaves "shore's end" for the ocean of Infinity and the Absolute. "The one who truly wants to philosophize," he writes, "must be free of all hope, all desire, all aspiration, must not will anything, not know anything, but feel completely bare and impoverished, must give away all to win everything." They must, he explains, "at one time have abandoned everything, and themselves have been abandoned (*Verlassen*) by everything." This is a kind of death, and here Schelling thinks at once of Plato's *Phaedo* (philosophy as practice for death, which is to say, separation of the soul from the body) and of the biblical word (Mark 8:35) affirming that whoever wants to save his life will lose it. In this same text, *Ideas for the Philosophy of Nature as Introduction to the Study of the Sciences* (1821), he goes on to state provocatively that we should write on the threshold to philosophy Dante's inscription (in another sense, to be sure) posted above the gates of hell: "Abandon all hope you who enter here!" In these assuredly dramatic, even moving, statements, Schelling underscores that we can't have it both ways. We can't preserve the security and comfort of our quotidian certainties, while at the same time, by a kind of luxurious extension of our comfort zone, incorporate the original light of truth. In matters of meaning, philosophy goes all in. To those who see philosophy as an over-the-counter antidepressant without side-effects allowing us to enjoy the splendor of our egoistic selves with ever greater satisfaction, this page of Schelling's might be prescribed as a cure for denial.

In the language of the great German mystics, such as Eckhart, Tauler, and De Suso, who are the source of inspiration for others on this theme, in particular the French (Louis de Blois, who was cited extensively in the "Recollection" chapter, wrote *Apologia pro Johanne Taulero* ["A Defense of John Tauler"]), abandonment is expressed in the perfect participle of the verb "letting go" (*lassen*), *gelassen*, and the word, so rich in history, of *Gelassenheit* (*gelâzen* and *gelâzenheit* in the old German). It combines two senses of abandonment in French, the abandonment *of . . .* and the abandonment *to. . . .* It is necessary to abandon the world and the self entirely to be surrendered over to a loving confidence in God. Renouncing and offering come in a couplet, and the admirable Brothers Grimm dictionary (authors of the famous fairy tales) notes well that the emphasis is sometimes placed too heavily on one meaning, sometimes too much so on the other. Depending on the context, French translations frequently occlude what is at stake in the same word. In his twelfth German sermon, Eckhart says that the man who stands in the love of God "must have abandoned himself and (have abandoned) the whole world." The Brothers Grimm highlighted the transition from the verbal to the adjectival use: those alone who have abandoned themselves "without a moment's hesitation" are truly "released" (*aleine gelâzen*). This releasement is a radically inward act, one that for Eckhart, as for those who follow him, is connected to "nobility" and freedom: only he who is released from self, deprived and relieved of himself, is truly free. Free for God—and through him.

This swirling abandonment spills over to sermon fifty-two's famous statement: "Pray to God to be free from God" (*wir gotes ledic werden*), where it must be understood that "God" is a relative name for the creature, like "Lord," that God was not "God" before the world's creation, and that whoever lives in God no longer refers to him by that name. With a sweeter aroma of orthodoxy, Angelus Silesius employs the term several times: "But to abandon even God is a self-abandonment (*Gelassenheit*) very few men comprehend" (*Cherubic Wanderer* II.92). Schelling, in the page just cited, likewise speaks of "letting go even God" (*selbst Gott lassen*). Nietzsche seizes on it for his transvaluation of morals (*The Gay Science*, IV.292). We can imagine the trouble and controversies that such a formula can provoke. And yet, the hyperbole of such dereliction has its own rigor: if abandonment leads to the noble poverty of freedom, if its root is the abandonment of the *I* and its possessions, including the possession of self-possession, it cannot but be understood as extending to "God," insofar as I appropriate it to myself, and still in some way possess it.

In Tauler, the self-renunciation of *Gelassenheit* often also has the sense of neglect and dereliction, a feeling of being forsaken by God and everything, which he calls an inner "winter" (Sermon 13), whereby Christ is more present than in the joyous "summer" of a tangibly felt presence. It is a conforming of oneself to Christ's humanity on the cross, a mysticism of Good Friday. It happens that the greatest generosity and sacrifice, as with Mother Teresa's in our time, finds its source there, paradoxically from a human point of view. The sense she had of "walking alone in darkness," the depths of which is evident in her letters, has troubled many, yet such an experience is a cornerstone of Christian mysticism.

Let us leave this altitude that an ordinary man such as the one penning these lines does not approach without circumspection. To what form of existence does this self-abandonment to God, this act of confidently relying on his will, lead? It leads to embracing things, events, and people as they come, and as they present themselves to us, with abandon (in the first sense of the term), with a receptivity that only the shedding of our own will makes possible. Not wishing in advance for this thing rather than that, the destitute man can't be disappointed by what comes to be. He seeks to discern the message God addresses to him, and the task presented to him here and now. The abandoned man lives a life of confident improvisation. For the freedom of self-renunciation is a liberation of the present as such (in the sense that the present is truly released). In the final chapter of his *Little Book of Truth*, Henry Suso asks the good question regarding the truly abandoned man (*reht gelazzener mensch*): "How does he comport himself to time?" He stands unfettered in the moment, taking from the smallest and greatest things alike what is "immediately necessary" (I thank Marc de Launay for suggesting this translation of *nehstes*, the superlative of *nah*.)

No writing has better emphasized the present moment than the literary and spiritual masterpiece of nineteenth-century French mysticism, *L'Abandon a la providence divine*, long attributed to Father Caussade, before being retracted on sound grounds (even though we know nothing of its author, not even his or her sex). Its model is the Virgin Mary's *Yes* to the divine will in the annunciation (Luke 1:38), an event she certainly could not have possibly expected, or prepared for in anticipation.

"The present moment is always like an ambassador declaring God's command, the heart always pronounces its fiat" (IX). The same chapter evokes "the present moment's divine fullness descending from the Father of Lights," after having already affirmed: "This present moment is always full of infinite treasures, contains more than what you can receive." Yet only self-abnegation is what opens access to this abundance: "In abandonment, the present moment is the unique rule. The soul is light as a feather, fluid as water, simple as a child" (IV). Or again: "All peering ahead that goes beyond this must be cut off, we must confine ourselves to the present moment without thinking either about what precedes or follows it" (III). And finally, the admirable conclusion: "The history of all the flowing moments is a holy history" (XI). We could never tire of citing such luminous sentences, which are as fluid as the life they describe.

Freed from all preference and premeditated designs through abandonment, man has a litheness that makes him entirely available for each situation's call. Philosophers, soothsayers, and strategists of ancient Greece scrutinized the moment (*kairos*), the favorable opportunity that must be seized by the reigns, without delay, for it only endures for a moment, between the "not yet" and the "too late," that right time to act and intervene. For the self-dispossessed, every present is an opportunity. What would be the use of straining to prepare myself to perform some courageous and generous act in the future if this very effort prevented me from seeing and doing what I can accomplish here and now, with respect to what comes first [namely, the present]? It would certainly be a total misunderstanding, however, to think that this emphasis on the now should lead to a form of hedonistic, however ethereal or distinct, enjoyment of the moment, or even a life released from all rules, doing what it pleases arbitrarily, and baptizing it as the call of God. The same treatise speaks of "pure duty" (II) and of "walking according to the right path of God's commandments" (IV).

There remain two serious questions to address regarding this abandonment. The one who renounces his own will and takes what comes as it arrives is without predilection; he accordingly is led to indifference, to what St. Francis de Sales in his *Treatise on the Love of God* (IX.4) examines at length under the moniker of "holy indifference." Besides the danger of quietism, a spiritual possibility of which it has always been suspected, often wrongly, though sometimes justifiably, doesn't it raise another undoubtedly even more disastrous danger, namely that of transforming Christian faith into a variant of stoicism? The eradication of all passion, "impassibility," constituted the stoic sage's ideal, and many a Greek monk's, albeit in a different context. Doesn't abandonment lead to this? The Brothers Grimm dictionary indicates quite clearly that the words *gelassen* and *Gelassenheit*, forged by the high mystics, appropriated by Luther and then by pietism, have been detached from their Christian foundation to assume a purely secular meaning of calm, of absence of disquiet (translated in French as "indolent, insensitive, indifferent, stoic"), then of composure and even coldness or lack of compassion, which can even be criminal (Goethe spoke once of a "monstrous indifference" in using *gelassen*!). Personal trust in a personal God has disappeared, there no longer being anyone to whom we can surrender ourselves. The most beautiful words can be devalued, even reversed into their opposites (*Gelassenheit*, for instance, becomes "nonchalance"). But Nietzsche himself will restore the word to its original meaning, by speaking uncharacteristically of "that sweet calmness (*Gelassenheit*) called 'prayer' that is a perpetual readiness for the 'coming of God'" (*Beyond Good and Evil*, 58), before even he unsheathes his claws. And Heidegger, referring to Eckhart in a complex, ambivalent, and somewhat backhanded fashion, delivered a lecture in 1955 entitled *Gelassenheit*, which has been translated into French as "Serenity," for lack of a better term. Yet is the transplantation of words to a private garden the remedy for their deracination, which is one of wandering's forms?

The second question obviously concerns surrendering to God's will: how do I access it? Can't I make the will of God in the present moment a convenient mask for my own whims, and perfect submission in principle in fact a very real disobedience? In the third of his *Entretiens spirituels*, "Trust and Abandonment," St. Francis de Sales distinguishes the "revealed will" of God (and thus the Bible and church ordinances and counsels) from the "will of his good pleasure," which concerns the unforeseeable events of life. The former is the norm for all discernment. Nonetheless, it remains the case that the life of abandonment requires a clear vision and more, not less, vigilance and lucidity than a perfectly regimented, organized, and

ABANDONMENT

pre-meditated life. Such a life's improvisation demands an intense sureness. For the act of self-abandonment there is no truth but in its flow: it is not something I can rely on, nor a title I can claim for myself. Its positive care-freeness has an evangelical origin: when inviting his disciples to cast off the cares of the pagans, Jesus enjoins them to seek first the kingdom of God and its righteousness, and everything else will be added to it. "Take therefore no thought for the morrow: for the morrow shall take thought for the things of itself. Sufficient unto the day is the evil thereof" (Matt 6:33–34). But the present's primacy is biblical only if it has justice as its horizon, and so in turn the radical future which happens here and now.

This self-renunciation of which the mystics speak is for most of us only a very distant high peak, from which so many obstacles separate us that we might be discouraged and tormented by having no experience of it, the anguish itself of not being abandoned driving us further away from abandonment rather than drawing us closer to it. Yet there is an abandon-ment that we can accomplish, or strive for, every evening. Namely, the self-dispossession of sleep. At the end of his admirable hymn to hope, *Le Porche du mystère de la deuxième vertu*, Charles Péguy discerns in this quotidian release in which we loosen the reigns of control, and accept that the world and things continue on their course without our intervention and surveil-lance, an act par excellence of trust in divine Providence. Owing to the impossibility of abandoning itself to God and others, insomnia violates the Gospel precept quoted just now (and all the more so as it is purer and more moral). It thus denies itself the secret resources upon which action draws from non-action, and its hypervigilance is a rope so taut that it eventually snaps at the expense, one way or another, of others. To fall asleep is to trust in the world, others, and God without protection (even if, to be sure, there is a depressive sleep that, as a flight into nothingness, reverses its meaning, and a slothful sleep that is merely sated animality). We're more capable than we hence think. And the sleeping body, by its very abandon, can have a grace and a beauty of no longer watching itself, where in the same glow its splendor and fragility are at once both manifest.

Meditation 10

Wound

THE WORD *BLESSURE* ("WOUND") is singularly French, its Frankish root sharing nothing in common with the other forms of designation found in the other Western European languages (*Wunde, wound, herida, ferida, ferita*). It refers at once to the act that inflicts it, the lesion it causes, and the suffering that sometimes remains with us for the rest of our lives. Yet, when we move from actuality to possibility, we are returned to the Latin's *vulnérable* and *vulnérabilité*. Bernard of Clairvaux, meditating on the misery of the human condition, saw in this domain's reality the condition of the possible. For him, in a word, we are only wounded because we are vulnerable, yet vulnerable because we are originally wounded: "We are wounded when entering, living in, and departing the world" (*Various Sermons*, 42.2). As for knowing if our wounds make us more or less vulnerable than before, weaker or stronger, we'd be inclined to say that this is the whole question, one posed by our wounds to which we must respond by our actions, if further reflection didn't soon reveal that it's misleadingly posed. For it may be that the fragility opened up within us by our wounds becomes the space of our greatest strength, just as the hardness we pride ourselves over having conquered is sometimes the beginning of our inhumanity, but also our blindness and presumption, those elusive agents of our downfall.

Our wounds, and the scars and infirmities they leave us, are ours, and allow us to identify and recognize ourselves. Having been rendered unrecognizable magically by the goddess Athena, it is by his timeworn wound that his old nurse recognizes Ulysses back in Ithaca (*Odyssey*, XIII.397) and, her spirit filled with both joy and sorrow, overturns the cauldron where she was washing his feet (XIX.467). It was before the wounds of his passion that

94

the apostle Thomas recognized the risen Jesus, despite the new condition of his body (John 20:25–28). Yet, even in the words that we hear, the inflection of the voice that cracks at certain words or names would be to us, even in the night, as sure a sign of recognition, and the soul has its wounds just as much as the body. Should we always seek to heal them? Let us recall the powerful statement of Hegel's Jena notebooks from 1803–1806 that asserts that, although a hemmed stocking is better than one torn, the same cannot be said for self-consciousness. The pages here to follow will focus on these wounds, those not meant to be healed but rather to be blessed, for they were the breaking through of what is higher into our being, or the opening within it of its noblest destiny. It is still necessary, certainly, to agree on what it means not to be cured of it: it is not a question of languishing in a romantic and doleful attitude, as with Baudelaire's beautiful and deleterious reverie ("Former Life," *Flowers of Evil*), with "his naked slaves, impregnated with fragrance," "And whose sole concern was to deepen / The secret grief in which I languished." (These verses conclude the poem: by drilling into it, they render the pain even more exquisite—for this word's significance, consult your dentist—the secret, by its very evocation, can only be contained in love.) Stronger possibilities are at stake here.

The biblical example par excellence of such wounds is the "thorn in the flesh" of St. Paul, who mentions it in the Second Letter to the Corinthians (12:7–10). To purge him of all pride, he says, "there was given to me a thorn in the flesh, the messenger of Satan to buffet me." "For this thing I besought the Lord thrice, that it might depart from me. And he said unto me, 'My grace is sufficient for thee: for my strength is made perfect in weakness.'" The empty curiosity of commentators has elicited a long catalog of physical or psychic ailments, from epilepsy to malaria, pertaining to the nature of this "thorn"; some have gone so far as to consult dilettante and idle doctors (Doctor Watsons of exegesis) from whose clinical data it is hard to see what could be concluded. In the beautiful reflection that he dedicates to this passage (it is the second of his *Four Edifying Discourses* of 1844), Kierkegaard had already criticized this idle chatter, and justifiably laid emphasis on the fact that this apostolic word stands, in essence, within a dimension whereby what concerns one individual man concerns all others, and so there is nothing that we cannot learn from our existence by the light of this very word (otherwise, what would be the use?).

What St. Paul is saying is that he was not as he would have wished, but as God saw fit, and that the rejection of his request was the actual answer to his prayer, as many spiritualists have noted. The wound of which he would have wanted to be healed, not for his ease of comfort, but because he perceived it as an obstacle or a difficulty in the way of his task, will have been, by the grace of God, a source of strength and active abundance—through the very acceptance of his continued vulnerability. And the lesson here that St. Paul provides (one of the most unforgettable of his) is not one that he himself has conceived and composed, but one that the painfulness and the wounding (both because of the very persistence and the repeated rejection of his request) has given to and imposed on him violently, and that has taken him by surprise, and set him back. As Kierkegaard says well, by this very fact, the "Angel of Satan," whatever it may be, is transformed into a messenger of God. It is, moreover, extremely important that this thought about the wound becoming a grace and a blessing should not be taken up in general considerations, like a prayer for the proper use of illnesses, but in an account that evokes a singular wound and its fuller fruit. This is why the invocation of the thorn as a biographic element, just as the fact that it remains in its indeterminate nature, is part of the passage's very economy, and the significance of its teaching. Blessed thorn that showed us the burning word of God has unfolded through the very weakness of Paul! (Note that in the biblical Greek, St. Paul's seldom-used word usually refers to others who stand in the way of our goal, like brambles on the path.)

There are not only words about wounding, but also wounding words. We all know, to our own detriment and chagrin, that a word can wound more deeply (and more permanently) than a slap or a blow—and more cruelly, too. It is words of insult and humiliation that open wounds in our hearts that can be difficult to heal, and that sometimes never do. The grotesque dictum according to which "only the truth hurts" suggests that the abuser or slanderer, not content with having hurt us, uses our very suffering as a further argument against us, and by this sophism transforms his cruelty into an apparent triumph of justice and morality. Add to boot the saying, "he who apologizes, accuses himself," and we are prisoners without recourse. Some commit suicide because they cannot endure the infamy of a baseless accusation thrown against them, and the very idea of having to defend themselves in its face feels like a stain and dishonor.

Yet the word that wounds is not always one of insult, nor uttered by a fellow human being. Hence, for example, in Stendhal's *The Red and the Black* (I.11), the word "adultery" appears suddenly in Madame de Rênal's consciousness, and forces her to see her relationship with Julien Sorel in a terrible light, tearing her out from the darkness into which such bad faith plunges us when we fail to realize the meaning of our actions. There are also the word's joyous wounds, however, which can be those of God. In the painting exhibited at the Louvre, Perugino's graceful *Saint Sébastian*, though pierced by two arrows, does not seem at all affected. In a perfect state of serenity, his head thrown back, and already ringed with a halo of holiness, he lifts his eyes heavenward, with an expression of intense attention.

Does he see and hear things that we ourselves do not? In any event, he doesn't call for help. At the bottom of the table, as if cut out in capital letters, appears the Latin phrase: *Sagittae tuae infixae sunt mihi* ("Your arrows are aimed at me"). It originates from Psalm 37:3 [in the Vulgate] (38:3 in the Hebrew [and 38:2 in the English]), the supplication of the sinner weighed down by his faults who calls for God's help. In the context of the Psalms, these arrows are those of God's wrath and chastisement. But, as so often is the case, the expression has been detached from its context and enriched with other meanings. For the Christian tradition, these arrows become the words themselves of God, and not simply words of reproach or of judgment.

Speech becomes an arrow when it wounds and pierces us, when it penetrates to the very depths of our being, when we can no longer distance ourselves from it, when we can't tear it away from us (at least not without tearing ourselves apart, or creating a worse wound that would have nothing beneficial about it). A piercing word is one that we not only can't pretend we haven't heard, but that continues to lodge within us, to act upon us, and to transform our own presence to ourselves and to others. Yet these arrows can be loving. For St. Augustine, this word concerning the word of God and its efficacy is decisive. An indication of this is the evocation of these arrows in a central passage of the *Confessions* (IX.II.3), when St. Augustine, abandoning the teaching of rhetoric, prepares to retire with his friends in order to meditate on and pursue the truth: "You had pierced our hearts like arrows with your charity, and your words were planted in our bowels." He also develops its significance in relation to the "sharp arrows" evoked in another psalm. The latter, he says, "are the words of God. Behold, they are launched and pierce hearts: but when hearts have been pierced by the arrows of God's word, it is love that is aroused, not death that is brought about. The Lord knows well how to shoot arrows for love: and no one shoots arrows for love more beautifully than he who does it by the word. Better still, he pierces with arrows the heart of the lover, to help the lover: he pierces with arrows to give us love. When we act with words, they are indeed arrows" (*Exposition on Psalm 119.5*). (Note that, like in the text quoted from the *Confessions*, if arrows do not suffice, burning coals are required, which he then goes on to explain, but they are always wounds.)

If the wound these arrows of words inflict on us is the wound of love, it is clear that it is a blessed wound, one that enlarges and expands our life, and the worst thing we could do would be to seek to heal ourselves from it. Images besides an arrow can evoke with equal power this initial wound, which it would be fatal to try to close. Thus, in Canto XXVI of *Paradise* when Dante, the sojourner through the afterlife, is asked about his love of God, the question is put to him in these unexpected terms: "Let us hear / from what teeth this love has come to you" (50–51), and in his reply evokes "each of the bites / that can turn hearts to God" (56–57). Colloquial French not long ago rediscovered this wound when speaking of being "bitten," of being smitten, or passionate. Some interpreters detect only remorse here; but when Dante describes these bites, they are encouraging acts, not reproaches, of God the Creator and Savior. It is Love indeed that bites, even if this leads undoubtedly to a change of life.

The short biblical word that gave its greatest impetus to Christian mysticism in this respect is the Song of Songs (2:5): "For I am sick of love." Where precisely the Vulgate and modern translations speaks of love's "sickness" or "longing," the Septuagint, following the fathers, speaks instead of a "wound." Augustine situates this word in relation to the arrows just mentioned, saying, "Whoever has not been wounded by this wound cannot reach true holiness" (*Exposition on Psalm 37:5*). In every sense of the term, love is a "beneficial wound." Origen uses this expression in his *Commentary on the Song of Songs* (Prologue.II.17), and, as in so many other instances, he was the first to develop magnificently the thought of such a wound. We all know the imagery of young Eros casting his arrows haphazardly, and thereby causing great disasters, but the divine Archer is neither blindfolded nor mischievous, and knows very well what he does, and why. The one, says Origen, who has been struck by this "sweet wound" (*dulce vulnus*) topples over into the love of the Word in such a way that nothing else occupies him (*Commentary* III.8.13). Yet this inaugural exposition has a richness of its own that won't always be present in subsequent accounts.

Throughout his work as a whole, Origen emphasizes the wide variety of names and figures of Christ: the Shepard, but also the Lamb, the Way, the Door, and so forth. These names represent the many faces with which he can appear to us, depending either on our personality and orientation, or according to our steps along the spiritual path. In the most extensive passage on love or charity's wound (III.8.15), he treats it as a generic name. When we are wounded by the Word of God, it is always love that wounds us. But this wound can assume different figures, and it is this or that feature of the Word that constitutes for us the tip of its arrow: the soul (in the figure of the Song's beloved) can be "wounded by wisdom," or "wounded by force," or "wounded by justice," to name just a few. The loving wound is accordingly multifaceted, and its effects are not always identical. Even if Origen does not go into detail, confining himself to enumerating the ways by which God can wound us, we can imagine two main possibilities. In the first (which obviously is the one to which he adheres), I am wounded in the place itself of my deepest desire, and this is why the lover is a man who above all is in love with justice, and who is transfixed by a glimpse of divine justice, which only makes his upright heart palpitate all the more. In the second, the wound can be understood as striking me where I am not expecting it, through my "mistakes," as Péguy says of grace, and therefore where I need it most to open up to a dimension that till then had remained closed to me, or even unsuspected (think of St. Paul's conversion). In any case, for Origen, the "loving wound" is an event far too varied than the highly narrow sense this term will take on in later mysticism. That the Word himself is an arrow that pierces us is a notion Origen borrows from the prophet Isaiah: God "has made me a polished arrow; he has hidden me in his quiver" (49:2) (for Origen, it is an "elected" or "chosen" arrow), and the same passage also evokes speech: "he has made my mouth like a sharp sword."

Yet it is not just divine love that can wound us: there are also the arrows of evil and of Satan (*Commentary*, III.8.16–17). Sometimes, says Origen, they are so subtle that we do not even realize we've been affected by them, and the grief they cause is so faint that we don't pay them notice. Just as in the physical world, so too in the case of infectious diseases of the soul, it is sometimes the most fatal that fester for a long time without painful symptoms. A mosquito of a simple thought can lose us. In order to guard ourselves against them, as Origen goes on to say, the only means of being completely covered is the "shield of faith."

The expression comes from St. Paul in the Letter to the Ephesians (6:16): "Above all, taking the shield of faith, wherewith you shall be able to quench all the fiery darts of the wicked." The image of the "shield" was already prevalent throughout the Psalms, where it is God himself who is our protector. There is more depth here than initially appears to be the case: if we need a shield, it is precisely because our body is vulnerable to evil's assaults, and because it would be as illusory as it would be prideful to think that our own resources suffice to guard us. That we fancy ourselves invulnerable is already evil's first victory and wound, through which it introduces into us its fifth column, and gains headway on the spot, unbeknownst to us. That faith is the shield implies that we do not give it to ourselves, but that we hold on to it. For St. Paul, we do not merely have the defensive arm of the shield; we have also the offensive weapon of "the sword of the Spirit, which is the word of God" (6:17). In mutual love, the weapons that wound can change hands, as is common: the "two-edged sword," the living sword of the Word of God that penetrates us deeply to analyze us finely and reveal us to ourselves (Heb 4:12), is the same one that is entrusted to us in order to fight. And if the Word is the archer, we ourselves also have the bow of our desire: in *Paradiso* (XXVI.22–23), St. John asks Dante who aimed his bow at such a target, the target being God himself.

If love wounds, and deeply so, it is because it constitutes a joust, a struggle, even a battle, a common aspect of human and divine love's language. The word itself "war" very frequently appears in the love poetry of Petrarch, for example. And love's violence is furthermore the source of innumerable oxymorons (expressions where opposites meet) that are signatures of all loving speech: the wound that heals, the imprisonment that frees, the suffering that is sweet. . . . One of the most admirable medieval writings on love is the short work of Richard of St. Victor's twelfth-century *The Four Degrees of Violent Love*. The beautiful passage of St. Gregory the Great's *Morals on the Book of Job* (VI.25.42) concerning love's wound furnishes a perfect illustration: "indeed, God kills in order to sustain life, and strikes in order to heal: in other words, he uses exterior blows to heal the inside." And when the external blows cease, "he inflicts wounds within, piercing the shells of our minds with its desire (*mentis nostrae duritiam*)." "With the arrows of his love, God pierces spirits that have become insensitive, and immediately makes them, through his charity's ardor, capable of feeling." This is how he interprets love's wound from the Song of Songs. The soul "is marvelously revived by its wound, which before lay dead in health. She burns, she pants (*anhelat*), and now desires to see the one she's been fleeing."

Here to shake us from our torpor, our security, our anesthesia, is nothing less than love's violence. As for the "sigh," which later became a cliché of the most banal poetry, it clearly shows that the source of amorous oxymorons is itself oxymoronic; the lover speaks, and must speak, of the very thing that initially rendered him mute by taking his breath away, and so it is with breathlessness and with breathless words that he bounds from one song to another, and one poem to another. Constantly losing breath is what alone gives breath anew. We only need open at random the great poets of profane love to find St. Gregory the Great's oxymorons. "The same eyes that bore the wound can heal the wound," says Petrarch (*Canzoniere*, I.75). And Ronsard, in the *Les Amours* of 1552–53 (64), says of those who will visit his Lady ("Whom the vulgar call my mistress"): "He'll learn how Love rides & bites, / How it heals, how it gives death." In warfare of this sort, there is no shield, no "*écu*" (which comes from the Latin *scutum*). Petrarch evokes this "blow" of the gaze, "wearing neither helmet nor shield" (I.95). And Ronsard, in the *Second livre des Mélanges* (13), says of love's arrow: "But guard (= fortify) my heart against whom I have not sealed it, / Of whose features would crack a strong breastplate." This incessant circulation between erotic and mystic language, between human and divine, is in our tradition based on the Song of Songs, but the great Persian mystics will recognize it in their own way, and the Platonic *Eros*, which begins in the body and finite being, opens up a literally metaphysical dimension.

Nevertheless, this does not mean that these two languages of wounding are simply mirrors. Arriving at the ninth heaven, near the end of his ascent, Dante is astonished at the inversion this "metaphysical" heaven represents in relation to the physical heaven of the cosmology of his time: in the latter, in fact, the least noble, the earth, is at the center, and the further we move away from it, passing from one heaven to another (conceived as concentric spheres), the more we rise in dignity and beauty, whereas in paradise, God is at the center, and the circles of angelic light that dance around him are all the more noble for being closer (*Paradiso*, XXVIII.46). For Richard of St. Victor's *The Four Degrees of Violent Love* (19–20), there is a chiasmus or an inversion between that of human and divine loves: with the latter, the deeper and sharper the wound and violence, the better, whereas with the former, which is excellent in itself, when its violence increases, there's a veritable descent into hell (he goes so far as to speak of an image of "future damnation" in relation to love's madness: it is a season in hell). He is describing romantic love. Why this inversion? Why does the severity of the love-wound have an entirely different meaning, it being understood that it is in no way a deprecation of human love?

The captivating (in the strict sense), obsessive, exclusive character of a love culminating to a point whereby nothing else suffices, in a devouring insatiability whereby unquenchable desire swirls, removes us from all our duties, from all our tasks, leaves us no space within ourselves for anything other than to be loved, and becomes, when it is a question of human love, in the very sharing of love, a torture without recourse, and madness without remedy. By contrast, in divine love, the exasperation of loving suffering transforms and shapes us in such a fashion that we instead become perfectly supple and generous in fulfilling our duties to others, and more so than our duties, the mark of this love being letting go to the divine will. Beyond a certain point, love's wound encloses us in a way we never could have been otherwise but for it, or else it frees us, giving us a receptivity that we never could have received without it. Depending on what produces it, the enormity leads us in one of these two opposing directions.

The great mystics of the Spanish Golden Age, St. Teresa of Ávila (to whom we will confine ourselves here) or St. John of the Cross, will carry to a kind of summit or pinnacle the meditation on and diction of love's wound. Summit also means that it tends to become a specific mystical phenomenon, situated at the highest stages of the spiritual journey, whereas in what has been mentioned so far, it has a broader meaning, one that everyone can by right experience. Gregory the Great insisted on the fact that love begins with wounding (even if, of course, it will deepen by taking other forms), and for Richard, *caritas vulnerans* (the love that wounds) was only the *first* stage among the four of which he distinguishes.

The wound of love (*esta herida del amor*) described by the great Teresa of Ávila was made visible, to the point of misunderstanding (as with all celebrity), even to those who didn't read her, by Bernini's[1] mid-seventeenth-century masterpiece in the Cornaro Chapel of Rome's Church of Santa Maria della Vittoria. Integrated perfectly into the architecture from which it was conceived, as well as the lighting, it shows us St. Teresa in ecstasy, carried atop a cloud which seems firmer and heavier than herself. From the extraordinary whirlwind of her garment's thousand folds, there emerges her bust which still has the strength to rise up, her face turned upside down, eyes nearly closed, mouth half-open and absent from the world, which contrasts with her relinquished hanging hand (the left, of course). Above her, gazing down, is a graceful, smiling angel aiming a golden arrow at her. The aged Bernini, it is said, used to come and pray before the altar above which his work is displayed—as what we make makes more sense than we ourselves. But if the Baroque painter very often featured saints in ecstasy, the sculpture's theme is exceptional, and represents a kind of challenge. Bernini closely followed an account of the saint from chapter 29 of her *Life*.

---

1. Gian Lorenzo Bernini (1598–1680), Italian sculptor and architect, who is considered the inventor of Baroque style.

The extremity of pain, which leaves only breath for her groanings, goes hand-in-hand with the excess of the sweetness. The soul, she says, cannot then be content with less than God. Love's wound is desire's incandescence (the tip of the arrow, she explains, is the fire), and not its extinguishment in satisfaction: this flame of desire remaining desire is what leads Teresa to say elsewhere that she is dying not to die. The sculptor chose one of the stories that best portrayed him. Yet she herself specifies that a vision of an angel (quite different from a feeling of one's presence) was rare for her. In any event, it is not a question of just one scene, and his work affords other depictions, in which the visible is effaced into the pure suffering heart. The Bernini grouping connects cause and effect in the simultaneity of the plastic work: the angel's gesture appears to be that of shooting an arrow, yet the saint has already been wounded, and no longer sees him. This is what we call its transverberation, the dart of love's piercing it.

In the spiritual *Relationships* (*Cuentas de conciencia*, 54), she mentions a pain that is like that of the arrow, yet adds that sometimes this wound comes from within, from "the soul's intimacy," and furthermore puts emphasis on desire as such. In the *Interior Castle* (VI.11.2), she speaks of that which is like "a flaming arrow" (*una saeta de fuego*) by specifying: "I do not say that this is an arrow," and at once insists on the interiority of this suffering. This chapter gives the longest description of it, apt to denigrate (if they wanted to, though they do not) those who gloss over the undeniable sensuality of Bernini's sculpture. This wound strikes us with powerlessness, it accomplishes what mysticism calls the "ligation of the powers," which is to say, the faculties of the soul, without being annihilated, do no more than endure this wound. The wound in question is purifying, says Teresa, striking us like lightning in order to consume everything that is not love, and she compares its torment to the pains of purgatory. We are far from joyousness! It is an ordeal, an interior martyrdom. For this reason, this exceptional event only occurs in the vicinity of the summit.

Over and over again, St. John of the Cross (for example, in the *Spiritual Canticle*, 13.9) insists upon the reciprocal or mutual character of love's wound, whereby the divine Love is itself wounded as well (what else is the passion of Christ?). The wound of love is the wound of desire, and desire grows with love, always deepening the wound itself. The shortness of breath also increases as we approach the summit and its great height. And the greatest masters in this order do not provide us balms or palliatives, but the joyful and serious good news that the wound may be incurable.

www.ingramcontent.com/pod-product-compliance
Lightning Source LLC
Chambersburg PA
CBHW032233080426
42735CB00008B/831